Sometimes
You Just Need
More Money!

- Is financial stress taking a toll on your family?

- Does one income come up short, no matter how many coupons you clip or how much you slash your budget?

- Would a higher income for your husband allow you to spend more time with your kids?

- Do you think your husband is not getting the salary he deserves?

- Is money the deciding factor in whether you stay home—rather than your personal desires?

- Would having you at home be best for your entire family?

If you answered yes to any of these questions, then this guidebook is for you. In HOW TO HELP YOUR HUSBAND MAKE MORE MONEY, SO YOU CAN BE A STAY-AT-HOME MOM, you will learn strategies that can help move your husband up the ladder, simplify his job search, and raise his earning power. Whether he spikes his income where he works now or moves on to greener pastures with a better, higher-paying job or a successful business of his own, your new-found expertise will support him in his efforts and afford you the opportunity to enjoy your own full-time career—raising your kids!

How to Help Your Husband
Make More Money
So You Can Be a Stay-at-Home Mom

Joanne Watson

WARNER BOOKS

An AOL Time Warner Company

This book was previously self-published by the author under the title *Team Work*.

Warner Books, Inc., 1271 Avenue of the Americas, New York, NY 10020
Visit our Web site at www.twbookmark.com.

 An AOL Time Warner Company

Printed in the United States of America

First Warner Books Printing: January 2003

10 9 8 7 6 5 4 3 2 1

Library of Congress Cataloging-in-Publication Data

Watson, Joanne.
    [Team work]
    How to help your husband make more money so you can be a stay-at-home mom / by Joanne Watson.
        p.cm.
    Originally published: Team work / by Joanne Watson. Glendale, CA : Family Books, 2001.
    Includes bibliographical references and index.
    ISBN: 0-446-69016-3
    1. Married people—Finance, Personal. 2. Husbands—Employment. 3. Motherhood. 4.Wives—Effect of husband's employment on. 5. Work and family. I. Title.

HG179 .W329 2002
332.024'0655—dc21

                                                        2002069022

Book design and text composition by H. Roberts Design
Cover design by Tom Tafuri

To the mothers and children of the world,
and to my three inspirations for being
a stay-at-home mom—
Brian, Brandon, and Rebecca—
and my husband, Patrick

Contents

Introduction

Although I adore my husband—after all, he is funny, smart, charming (at least on his good days), and is one of my best friends as well as being my devoted partner—making money was not his strong suit.

My husband's income just did not cover our expenses.

So, like many women across America, I was faced with what to me was a horrible choice; going to work full-time outside the home to add to my husband's income.

Horrible, because I really loved being a mom, full-time. I think it is the best job around.

No other job comes with benefits that even compare to being there to see those first steps, receiving that spontaneous hug in the middle of the day from your toddler as she tells you "I love you very so much!" or watching the smile spread across your son's face as you help him mas-ter 4th grade math.

As I watch the progress of my children, I would have to give my overall job satisfaction and sense of accom-plishment a 10.

I determined that there was no way that I could do it. I just could not leave my children at day care. It wasn't for me.

What were my alternatives? Living on less? Not very likely, since the cost of living where we lived was high, and we didn't want to leave our friends and family. Not hav-ing enough money to have a good savings plan for emer-gencies was not my idea of security for the family either.

Work from home? It might work, but it wasn't the best solution, since we needed a guaranteed additional income, and not all small businesses are profitable quickly (or ever, for that matter). I also preferred to be able to devote my time and attention to the raising of my chil-dren, and working from home would take a lot of that precious time away.

But we did need more money. There had to be another way.

Thinking about the situation, and remembering some reading I had done at my church about marriage and dealing with problems, it occurred to me that if I helped my *husband* make more money, then I could have what I wanted: to be a stay-at-home mom *and* have more money. After all, we were a team.

I set out to help him, figuring that the time I invest-ed in helping him was much less than the time I would be away from my family if I was earning the money personally.

And, step by step, I helped my husband to make more money.

I used techniques that I share with you in my book. Some things I knew to do, others I found out about. I researched, and researched, and I talked to people (some of whose stories are in the book), and I put into practice actions that I felt would help our team.

The result was that my husband's income increased by over 300%, and I am at home with my children.

Many women have had to decide what to do about their financial situation and the care of their children, but there was a piece of the puzzle missing.

For women who wanted to be stay-at-home moms, there were books on how to live on less money and how to work from home, but there were no books on how to work as a team with your husband to get the life that you want.

Looking around at other mothers and children, I felt an obligation to pass on some of what I knew, so that other women could have the opportunity to experience the joy and fulfillment of being a stay-at-home mom, and their children could receive all the benefits of having them at home full-time.

If we were sitting down over a cup of tea, and you asked me how you could be a stay-at-home mom and still have more money, this is what I would tell you.

How to Help Your Husband Make More Money So You Can Be a Stay-at-Home Mom

Chapter 1

The "Team Work" Decision: Great Ideas Come Before Great Actions

The First Step

Is your secret (or not so secret) desire to be a stay-at-home mom? If so, you are NOT alone. Many working mothers would prefer to stay home with their children, *if their husband's income alone could support the family.*

A growing number of women feel that it is better for children to have their mother at home, and many women are finding that needing to work full-time outside the home is a source of stress in their relationship with their husbands.

Despite these facts, many woman are working outside the home full-time in response to the need for more money to support the family.

The alternatives of trying to work from home or live on one paycheck that is too small aren't always workable or desirable. Working at home is not for everyone. Cutting back on expenses is not always a solution. Sometimes there are financial obligations that just have to be met, like medical expenses or mortgage payments.

If this is your situation, does it mean that you will just have to try to "make the best of it" and resign yourself to giving up your dream of being a stay-at-home mom?

Absolutely not. There is another option, but it is a bit of a lost art.

In today's high-speed Internet-connected world, **it is easier than ever to help your *husband* make more money, *if you know how.***

Often times, despite both parents working outside the home full-time, couples find that they are "just getting by" and are no closer to being able to realize their stay-at-home-mom goal. Meanwhile, neither parent is home with the children.

On the other hand, helping your *husband* to make more money is an approach that has helped many women to successfully afford to stay home with their families, while strengthening the family unit.

But how do you help your husband make more money?

You do it by approaching your family's income using the Team Work concept. Using the Team Work concept, you form a *team* with your husband and take an *active* role in his success.

Team Work is about taking responsibility for your relationship, working together—yet in different ways, each part contributing to the whole and using a loving and supportive approach to building the life you want.

Using Team Work will help build your income and your relationship.

Most men have the desire to make more money, and many of them share in the feeling that it is better for children to have a stay-at-home mom, and would like to make enough money for their wives to be home with the children if they could do so.

And whether they will tell you or not, many men find that it is a source of personal frustration, as well as stress in their relationship with their wife, that their wife needs to work full-time outside the home to make ends meet.

However, without guidance on *how* to make enough money to be able to afford to have their wife stay home with the children, and for lack of a better alternative, the situation continues.

In *How to Help Your Husband*, you will be taken step-by-step through the actions that can give you the life you want, **but the decision is up to you.**

Those precious years when your children are young will go by all too fast. Don't sit on the sidelines watching the life you want pass you by. The difference between looking back with regret and looking back with a sense of fulfillment starts with your decision.

Without changing your mind, you will not change your circumstances.

The first step is for you and your husband to make the decision to work together as a team to turn your stay-at-home-mom goal into a reality.

The Strength of Team Work

One person working alone can accomplish a certain amount. Two working side by side can accomplish more. But two working as a *team* is the most effective way to accomplish your goals.

Imagine a football team that was made up of all quarterbacks. Or a baseball team that was made up of all second basemen, with no one to cover third, etc.

Yes, they would catch more balls thrown to second base than a team with only one second baseman, but there would be gaps in their coverage that would leave them vulnerable.

The same is true of the family. With both parents trying to "do it all" by working full-time outside the home and taking care of a family, they often say they can't do either as well as they would like.

However, by using Team Work to improve your income, you will have the advantage and strength of a team. With your help and support, your husband's odds of success increase, making it much easier for him to provide the kind of income needed for your family to achieve its stay-at-home-mom goal.

Using Team Work, each role in the family contributes to the success of all the other parts of the family. With Team Work, you can reclaim the family and its strength.

Use your resources in the most effective way possible by approaching your family's income with Team Work.

BRINGING UP THE SUBJECT

It is important to bring up the subject in a *positive* way. Let your husband know that you think he is a great guy, and that he is worth more money. Tell him you would like to work as a *team* to help him get the pay he deserves.

Explain to him that by pooling your resources, you increase your odds of success. You can remind him that his favorite football team or baseball team is made up of more than one player, and together they win the game.

Here is an inspiring quote he may relate to:

People who work together will win, whether it be
against complex football defenses, or the problems
of modern society.
—*Vince Lombardi, ESPN's Coach of the Century*

The truth is, if you are working outside the home currently, you are already helping with the family income—just in a more expensive way.

DO THE MATH

It is easier than most people think to raise their husband's income by enough to stay home with their children.

One important (but often overlooked) fact is that you don't have to replace your entire income to make it work. You only need to replace the part that you are keeping after deducting work-related expenses like child-care, office lunches, transportation, work wardrobe, etc.

So, for example, if you are a mom of two earning $30,000, and you are spending $15,000 on child-care and other work-related expenses, you would need to help raise your husband's income by only $15,000 in order to have the same net result, but with the added bonus of you being able to be home with your children.

If the change from two incomes to one lowers your tax bracket, you will have a savings there, too.

Of course, you will need to factor in the replacement cost of any job benefits you receive, as well, such as insurance provided by your employer, etc.

If you sit down and go over the numbers, you can figure out how much you really need to raise your husband's income by to accomplish your stay-at-home-mom goal. It may be less than you imagined. Either way, that amount then becomes Target #1.

It is best if you both agree on your target, so there are no misunderstandings, and you can keep your eyes on your goal.

Achieving your target may happen all at once, or it may come in stages, and it is important to celebrate your victories along the way, and acknowledge what you have achieved as a team.

Of course, once you have achieved and celebrated Target #1, you may want to set Target #2, which will allow you to achieve greater financial stability and help you to accomplish your other financial goals.

BELIEVE IN YOUR TEAM

Sure, you will have to apply what you have learned, and it will take some action on your part, but once you have made the decision and have the know-how, **it's really not that hard to do.**

A big part of success is believing in your ability to accomplish what you set out to do. A confident approach will open more doors than a timid one will.

Many people have successfully used these Team Work techniques to raise their husband's income—some of them with less skills than your team. If they can do it, so can you.

Being armed with the knowledge of how to go about something makes it a much easier task. For example, having a good recipe makes it a lot easier to bake a cake!

How to Help Your Husband will give you knowledge to confidently guide your path to the life that you want.

There are plenty of high-paying positions out there. Some of the top executives are making hundreds of millions of dollars a year. Do you think that all of them are that many times more qualified than most hardworking Americans? Neither do I. But they have accomplished something that they dreamed of, and they are being paid very well for it.

A "high" salary for your husband, one that by itself comfortably supports a family, is not too high of a goal to shoot for. It happens every day all over the country.

In any economy, opportunities exist. It is important for you to keep in mind that there are plenty of high-paying jobs out there. Employers and hiring managers are right at this moment grappling with the problem of how to find the right person to solve their particular problem and fill their need.

The idea that it is hard to do can be a self-fulfilling prophecy.

Decide that it is easy, follow the steps, and it soon will be.

Chapter 2

Assess Your Husband Through Rose-Colored Glasses

Never mind that your husband leaves his clothes out for you to put away (no matter how many times you remind him!), your husband has **great attributes**. *Find them and unlock the door to more income.*

To increase his income, you and he may need to effectively communicate what is really *great* and *valuable* about your husband, either by your husband to his present employer in seeking a raise or promotion, or to prospective employers, *or by you* to friends and acquaintances who may refer you to a great new opportunity for him. (More about that in Chapter 5.)

Learn to focus on the positive. Ignore the rest.

Become your husband's biggest supporter. That is part of Team Work.

Many times you will find that your husband has

valuable skills that *he* takes for granted if he is not being well paid for using them. Being underpaid can undermine his confidence in himself and make it harder to get a raise or a top-paying position.

LAYOFFS AND SETBACKS

What if your husband has had some setbacks? Maybe his company "downsized," or he lost a job, or just didn't get the job or raise he thought he should have.

Don't let him get stuck in the temporary "defeat." It's easy to focus the attention on setbacks, but you can help him put his attention on his past successes, and the ones he wants to create for the future.

By pulling together as a team, and encouraging him, you can make those "bumps in the road" seem like just that—part of the trip to his ultimate success.

Many successful men have overcome obstacles to get where they are. Walt Disney, for example, reportedly went bankrupt more than once before realizing his tremendous success.

Remember, the world is full of opportunities—those you find, and those you make. That holds true in any economy. There are always products and services that people need and want.

A lot of success has to do with confidence. By building your husband's confidence, you may build his income.

Everyone has terrific gifts and abilities. You want to bring out the best in your husband by validating those abilities, and helping him to focus on the positive.

Your husband's talents are special and unique to him.

ACTION PLAN:

1. **Write a list of things that he is good at.**

For example, is your husband really good with computers? Is he the one everyone in the office goes to if they have a problem they can't solve? There are many hi-tech careers that pay well enough to support a family.

Are there subjects that people come to your husband for advice on? It could be a "hobby" that leads to an excellent income source. People tend to do very well working in fields they really enjoy.

Don't allow false modesty to get in the way of a complete assessment. If your husband feels that some of his skills are at the beginner stage rather than the advanced stage, make sure that he doesn't take them for granted, *and write them down anyway.* You can make a note by them as to the degree of skill.

Those skills may be quite valuable to others just as they are, and *failing to acknowledge them may be costing your family money in terms of lost income.*

Additionally, they provide a foundation that can be expanded upon later to increase your husband's earning potential, so it is good to note them.

Try to make your list of skills as complete as possible. *Skills are assets.* It can help to have a good inventory of them. As you progress through the book, you will learn more about how to turn those assets into the money your family needs for you to be a stay-at-home mom.

2. **Add his experience to the list.**

Take stock of the different jobs your husband has had and the actual *functions* he performed. Sometimes employees end up with responsibilities far outside the position they were hired for. *Ignore the job title.* If he has actually performed tasks that are required in another job, *he has gained valuable experience and has other marketable skills* that you and he need to keep in mind.

Ask him about *accomplishments* that he is proud of, and *write down the top 5*. They will help demonstrate his skills and how valuable he is to an employer.

3. **Next, write down some of his best qualities.**

Is he patient and easy-going? Is he focused and determined? Is he methodical and persistent in working out solutions? Is he dependable? Creative?

As your list of skills and attributes grows, take a fresh look at your husband. Doesn't he seem like the kind of guy you would like to hire as an employer?

There are plenty of employers out there in need of people who possess the items on your list.

Don't forget to tell your husband what you think is great about him. We give our children praise and encouragement. Our husbands can benefit from it as well, and it will strengthen your relationship while raising your income.

You can now set your sights high. When you and your husband come to appreciate how truly great his attributes are, it will be much easier to go after a referral, a raise, a promotion, or a new, higher-paying job and get it.

SKILLS

EXPERIENCE

ACCOMPLISHMENTS

ATTRIBUTES

Chapter 3

Knowledge Is Power— And More Money!

One of the best routes to a higher income is learning a new, marketable skill to add to your list.

Whether your husband is working in an entry-level position, is an experienced executive (whose salary alone doesn't meet all your financial obligations), or is somewhere in between, adding a new skill can boost his earning power.

The same holds true for blue-collar workers and white-collar workers.

Most of us have heard of a wife "putting her husband through medical school" (or dental school), but what if you need a larger income without investing many years in training for a new profession?

There are many options available for training. Some of them are very fast, and yet the increase in pay the new skill will bring is lasting.

How Team Work Comes into the Picture

Using the Team Work approach to education, you can help your husband find the training that is right for him, and support him by making the time available for him to learn that new skill.

Your investment in time alone with the kids so that your husband can study can pay you back handsomely in the things you want: higher income and the freedom to be a stay-at-home mom.

Supporting your husband while he learns is not a new idea, although it is one that may have gotten lost in the frantic pace of having both parents working outside the home.

Many years ago, Sally used this Team Work technique with amazing results

Sally's husband worked at a tennis shoe factory. Expecting their first child, Sally definitely wanted to be a stay-at-home mom. Sally researched and found a drafting program that her husband, Tim, could take in the evenings (this was before the computer-aided drafting of today, when drafting was done by hand).

After a short time in night school, Tim was able to land a drafting job at about double what he was making previously.

It didn't stop there, however, as Tim then learned design while on the job in the aerospace industry as a draftsman, and ended up contributing to the design of the Apollo rocket. Quite a long way from tennis shoe factory to space program! (You could even say it was one small step for Sally, and one giant leap for Sally and Tim!)

Sally and Tim eventually had five children altogether, and were able to buy property on acreage in California (with horses) and still afford to have Sally be a stay-at-home mom.

If Sally had just gone to work to supplement their income instead of using that Team Work approach to the situation, their lives would have been much different. With Team Work, Sally and Tim used their resources in the most effective way possible.

Fast Training Options

There are many skills that can be learned quickly. Of course, only you and your husband can determine what is right for your team based on his interests, experience, and income requirements, but here are a few possible ideas:

There are quite a few computer courses that fit this bill

Learning to program Web pages for the Internet is a good example. Those skills can be learned in a few weeks or months, depending on where you study and your rate of study.

HTML, the primary language used to create websites, is very easy to learn. My 11-year-old son can do it. He learned it from a free tutorial on the Internet, and he has proudly sent his first Web page to our relatives, complete with animated graphics and links to other pages on the Web.

Java and JavaScript are additional tools for website creation that can be learned in a reasonably short time. Data base administrators are also in demand, and that is another skill that can be learned fairly quickly.

Many companies need help with adding e-commerce (business done through the Internet) to their existing business, along with their other hi-tech needs.

Local computer training centers usually have certification programs that vary from a couple of weeks to around seven months, and are scheduled for evenings or weekends to accommodate working adults.

Most centers will allow you to retake the course, if needed, until you pass the certification exam.

For a computer novice, a good "PC Boot Camp" that introduces you to the computer hardware and software is a good place to start. Those courses are generally short—about 16 hours or so, and run about $150–$250 in price.

What if your husband is not into computers?

Another good choice would be one or more of the short courses in Management Skills offered by the American Management Association.

The AMA offers self-study or seminar-style study courses in subjects like Finance, Project Management, Setting and Achieving Goals, Marketing, Human

Resources, Sales Management, Operations/Manufacturing Management, etc., that can be completed fairly quickly.

Most of their courses can be completed in a few weeks to two months part-time, but give their students lifelong skills that they can use to land a better-paying job in management.

For someone who is already a middle manager or executive, a course in Internet marketing may be the ticket to moving up to some of the hottest positions with their higher salaries.

Is your husband more of a "hands-on" type of guy?

Maybe he'd like to learn heating and air-conditioning technology, or he might enjoy being an electrician. Contractors/trade schools offer a lot of choices in these and similar areas.

There are many other options out there. You can search out the ones that are a good fit for your husband at your local community college, through the Internet, from trade associations for your husband's profession (or the profession he would like to have), and through your local phone book.

Trade associations can be a good source of information. Is your husband an electrician, a mechanic, a manager? Is he in marketing, human resources, sales? There are trade associations for almost every profession. They can usually recommend training classes, and some sponsor their own, or hold seminars on topics of interest, especially the hottest new skills in that industry.

You can locate the trade association for his chosen profession through the Internet or by calling the reference desk at your local library.

But What About the Cost?

Training options vary considerably in price as well as length of time. Many courses can be gotten for free on the Internet. Others are minimally priced through the Internet, community colleges, and private training centers. For a bigger investment, there are still other options.

In my local area, an HTML programming course is running about $220 from a private computer training center. Other similarly priced courses are offered.

Some of the more extensive courses are a few thousand dollars. For example, the Oracle Database Administrator program which is 3½ to 4 months in length one Saturday per week (with follow-up practice needed at home), runs about $2,500.

Prices vary considerably, so you should check around and get several prices before signing up (or deciding that it is too expensive). You may find a much better price.

American Management Association courses are *very* reasonably priced, especially considering the skills they teach.

Course prices range from about $159–$295 for

self-study courses to a much higher $1,495 for inten-
sive seminar-style courses. Membership is not
required, however, members receive a 15% discount on
self-study courses and other benefits. The membership
fee is currently only $45.

Want to spend even less?

Community colleges often have courses for around
$11 per credit for local residents. Their offerings may
or may not cover the area your husband is interested
in, but it is worth checking out their catalog.

Some Internet courses charge a fee, while others
are completely free. Some good sites to check are
www.free-ed.net and www.webmonkey.com.

Another low-cost option is your local bookstore.
There are many how-to guides available covering
everything from HTML programming for beginners
to how to do electrical wiring, to the latest book on
human resource management.

Want to find training that is totally free?

In addition to the free Internet courses, you can
always send your husband to the public library. The
reference librarian can help him in his search. The
books are free, and the quiet, undistracted environment may help him to study if your home is filled with
the happy sounds of a large family.

Most libraries are Internet connected as well. If you
don't own a computer, you can use the library to do
your Internet research, but there is usually a small fee.

A used computer can be picked up for as low as $100, though, and it may be a very good investment.

For free "hands-on" training, your husband might consider an apprenticeship under a skilled contractor or professional in the area of his choice. Some pros would welcome the unpaid help on evenings or weekends in exchange for sharing a little of their know-how.

Sometimes you can find a paid apprenticeship program. A paid apprenticeship is a way for your husband to earn money while learning.

DOES YOUR HUSBAND NEED A DEGREE?

A bachelor's degree, and even an MBA from an accredited university, can be earned from home, and in less time than you'd think.

A degree is definitely an asset, and having one *will* open some doors, therefore I will cover the easiest way for a working adult to get one, **but not having one does NOT have to stop your husband from earning a high enough income to allow you to be a stay-at-home mom.** If you learn a skill, no matter where or how you learn it, you can market that skill and be paid nicely for it.

Take Larry, for example, a very dear friend of mine. Larry is a computer programmer for a large company. He is currently paid $70 per hour, which translates to approximately $140,000 per year for full-time work. Larry has no degree. In fact, he never finished high school. Looking for a way to earn a good income, despite his lack of formal education, Larry taught himself two computer languages: COBOL and Powerbuilder, and began earning a much higher income.

There are some famous examples of successful men who did not have degrees:

Thomas Alva Edison
Bill Gates
Peter Jennings
Richard Branson
(Founder and CEO of Virgin Airlines)
Charles Lazarus
(CEO of Toys "R" Us)

And nine Presidents of the United States didn't go to college. They are:

George Washington	Abraham Lincoln
Andrew Jackson	Andrew Johnson
Martin Van Buren	Grover Cleveland
Zachary Taylor	Harry Truman
Millard Fillmore	

Don't let anything hold you back from achieving your goals!

THE FASTEST ROUTE TO A LEGITIMATE DEGREE

As a working adult with years of experience and knowledge accumulated on the job and through life experience, your husband will not be starting from scratch.

In fact, one of the ways to earn a legitimate degree *quickly* from an accredited university is by obtaining college credit for what you already know.

Many colleges will grant credit for passing scores on approved tests which are open to anyone who wants to take them.

The GRE (Graduate Record Exam) and the CLEP (College Level Examination Program) are examples of these. In fact, according to the CLEP website, 2,900 colleges and universities now award credit for satisfactory scores on CLEP exams.

Additionally, credit can sometimes be obtained for what you have learned through life experience. This is known as a portfolio assessment. Thomas Edison University is one college that will grant credit this way.

Credit can sometimes be awarded for fluency in a foreign language, on-the-job training, non-collegiate courses, and even self-study of and experience with your favorite hobby.

Some, or all, of your husband's degree can be earned through alternative credits. At Regents College in New York, an entire degree can be earned through testing at local test centers near your home.

In addition to the GRE and CLEP tests, Regents College Examinations are available that cover quite a few subjects. Their test results are accepted at many other colleges as well. You can contact them directly at 1-888-647-2388 to request a free information packet on their program.

Regents College is an accredited university and is a member of the University of the State of New York. Established in 1971, Regents College has issued more than 83,000 degrees since that time.

DISTANCE EDUCATION

If your husband needs more credits, or simply wants to learn a new skill and receive college credit for it, distance education can help make that possible.

Local colleges generally offer evening and weekend programs, but if your local college doesn't offer the courses your husband wants to take, or if he needs more flexible scheduling, distance learning is another good option.

College courses are offered through the mail (correspondence) or through virtual classrooms on-line. Some on-line courses offer real-time discussions and opportunities to interact with an instructor.

Many prestigious universities now have Internet-based curriculum, and will also give credit through exams, although some have minimum attendance requirements.

For a more complete listing of accredited colleges, with phone numbers and addresses that offer distance learning and credit by exam, pick up a copy of one of the books listed at the end of the chapter. Most should be available through your local bookstore or on the Internet at Barnesandnoble.com or Amazon.com.

LEARNING NEW SKILLS STRENGTHENS YOUR TEAM

Learning a new skill is an enriching experience personally as well as financially.

The increased confidence that a new skill can bring may be enough to help your husband get a raise or a higher-paying position. Not to mention the fact that he can now fill a need that employers may have.

The additional skills he learns may help him to succeed at his current job, leading to a raise or promotion, while helping him to qualify for other (better-paying) job opportunities as well.

Whether it's a short course in management, training as an electrician, learning programming from a book, or completing a degree, adding skills to your list is a terrific accomplishment that strengthens your team—and may change your life.

RESOURCES

Computer Training

Independents

Look in your local phone book under Computer Training for private training centers near your home. Check for Microsoft Certified training centers, Oracle training, Novell, Cisco, or others.

Chains
New Horizons Computer Learning Center
(250 locations)
www.newhorizons.com
1-800-PC-LEARN (1-800-725-3276)

ExecuTrain
www.executrain.com
1-800-90-TRAIN (1-800-908-7246)

Internet-Based Courses
www.free-ed.net
www.webmonkey.com

Management Training
American Management Association
www.amanet.org
1-800-262-9699

Society for Human Resource Management
www.shrm.org
1-703-548-3440

Help Locating Trade Associations
Check your local phone book and also try:
www.associationcentral.com

Reference Books
Encyclopedia of Associations: National Organizations of the U.S. (available at most libraries)

National Trade and Professional Associations of the U.S. 2000 (available at most libraries)

College Degrees
Regents College
www.regents.edu
1-888-647-2388

Thomas Edison University
www.tesc.edu
1-609-292-6565

Examination Programs
GRE Educational Testing Service
www.gre.org
1-609-771-7670

CLEP
www.collegeboard.org/clep
1-609-771-7865

Regents College Exams
1-888-RC-EXAMS (1-888-723-9267)

Further Reading
Distance Degrees by Mark Wilson, M.A. (available at www.collegeathome.com or 1-541-459-9384)

How to Earn a College Degree Without Going to College by James P. Duffy

Getting a College Degree Fast: Testing Out and Other Accredited Short Cuts by Joanne Aber, Ph.D.

Chapter 4

Is Your Husband Underpaid?

Your husband may already have the right job, but at the wrong pay, which could prevent you from being a stay-at-home mom.

Unfortunately, many employees do not know their real value in the "open market" or to the company that they work for, and are too easy-going about receiving lower compensation than they could be getting.

The first Team Work step you can take to help rectify this situation is to remind your husband of how great he is. Go over the list you made with him in Chapter 2 of his skills, experience, and accomplishments.

Next, do some research. If your husband is underpaid, it may help for you to tell your husband that he is worth more, but having that fact validated by an outside source may be the step that helps your husband realize to that you are correct, and that he should receive a higher pay for his work—and it will certainly be useful for convincing employers of that fact.

COMPENSATION AND SALARY SURVEYS

Compensation is an art, not an exact science, but there are some guidelines that will tell you whether your husband's pay is in the right ballpark or not.

A Salary Survey is usually a chart that lists different jobs in a particular area, and shows what the *average* pay is for that job. (See example page 42.)

Some are fancier than others and will break it down into the low-average, medium, and high-average compensation for each job.

There are modifying factors to watch out for, such as company size and part of the country that was surveyed.

Some surveys specify these things, but others do not, and you will have to make adjustments accordingly.

Some good places to find salary surveys are:

www.salary.com
www.careerjournal.com
www.jobstar.org

If you are not connected to the Internet, you can get written materials from your local library, but make sure they are up-to-date. The reference desk will be able to help you, or you can access the Internet from there.

Another place to research is the current advertised openings for a similar position to your husband's for someone with an equal amount of experience. (More on where to find those in Chapter 8.)

After looking at salary surveys, you will both have an idea of an average or "industry standard" for your husband's position, **however, each employee is unique and brings their own special skills and experience to the job.**

If your husband would be hard to replace because he has been with the company for a long time, or is "the only one who really knows what is going on" with some part of the business, *that adds to his value.*

Likewise, if the "average" person in his position has X numbers of skills, but your husband has X, plus is able to do Y, his particular value to the company may be *higher* than those in the salary survey.

A salary survey will at least help make sure your husband is not *below* the bottom line.

AN INTERESTING RESOURCE FOR THOSE ALREADY EARNING $50,000 OR MORE:

Futurestep (www.futurestep.com) is a website created by Korn-Ferry, one of the oldest and most famous recruiting firms with offices in New York, Los Angeles, and elsewhere.

On their website you can register and fill in a fairly

long questionnaire about your employment history, education, current salary (which must be $50,000 or above), etc., and their computer database will automatically give you their market valuation of what they think you would be likely to receive if you were to seek out a new position.

If your husband is in this category, he may be pleasantly surprised by the outcome of his market valuation.

ONE WAY EMPLOYEES CAN BE UNDERPAID

If your husband is working overtime on his job, but is being paid a salary that doesn't change whether he works overtime or not, and was told that he is an "exempt" salaried employee, make sure that he has not been misclassified. It wouldn't be the first time that it has happened.

In addition to the federal law, each state has its own laws on this issue, and it is in your best interest to find out what they are in your state.

In California, for example, in order to be exempt from receiving overtime pay under the executive exemption, the employee has to supervise a minimum of two other employees, and can spend no more than 20% of his time performing functions that would not be considered exempt.

An employer could call an employee an executive all day long, but if he doesn't meet the legal definition of exempt, he must be compensated for overtime hours at time-and-a-half.

To clarify whether your husband meets the federal criteria for exempt from overtime status, you can call the Department of Labor Wage and Hour Division referral line at 1-866-4USWAGE. They can answer your questions about the federal criteria, and if your state has a Department of Labor (not all states do), they can direct you to the office nearest you for information on your state's guidelines as well.

Know your rights and your employer's responsibilities, or you could be leaving a lot of money on the table.

How About a Raise?

OK, so let's assume you have determined that your husband *is* underpaid, and it is time to get that raise that will help you meet your stay-at-home-mom goal.

Using the Team Work approach, you can increase his odds of succeeding.

1. **Help him to be confident.**

   You can practice with him asking for the raise, and drill the possible responses and his come-backs, until he is comfortable and confident about the task.

   On the first run through, your husband may be shy or uncertain in the way he asks for a raise or responds to questions. It's much better to get through any awkwardness in a practice session with you than in the real situation.

As you continue to practice, your husband's confidence will build, and by the time you are done, he will be cool, calm, and collected. When he is all of the above, is happy with his responses, and sounds certain that he deserves the raise and his company should give him one, he is ready to ask his employer.

His chances of success will have increased greatly by your Team Work.

2. **Help him to be prepared.**

Using the research you did, and the list you made in Chapter 2, **you can help him prepare convincing documentation as to why he should have a raise now.**

Copy a page of the salary survey that applies to his job. Highlight the pay if it is out of line with what he is currently paid.

From the list you made in Chapter 2, highlight specific accomplishments *that have saved his company money or helped them earn more.* Write those down on another piece of paper in a way that he can present them to his employer.

Going into the meeting prepared will help him make his point, and improve his chances of "making the sale."

NEGOTIATING IS A SKILL THAT CAN BE LEARNED

You can pick up some good books on the subject for your husband. The more he knows about it, the more he will be in control of the negotiation and its outcome.

In addition to **being confident** and **being prepared,** when it comes to negotiating, your husband should try to **be creative.**

Rather than let negotiations stalemate if your husband and boss don't see eye to eye on the increase in base pay, your husband should be prepared to offer some alternatives, to keep the negotiations alive.

There are alternatives to an increase in base salary that may affect your overall income and expenses enough to make up for the difference in your husband's current base salary and the higher base salary he is asking for.

For example, if your family is not covered on your husband's insurance plan, adding them can save a lot of money that would be coming out of your pocket from **after-tax dollars.**

Performance bonuses for increased production may be an offer that is hard for an employer to refuse. After all, it means the company will be making or saving more money too, when your husband earns that bonus.

Paid training for a higher position, where your

husband's boss *would* see fit to pay him that higher salary, could be another option.

Use your creativity to come up with alternatives that could work for your family.

BE WILLING TO WALK AWAY

If your husband is holding on to a job where he is underpaid for dear life, as if it is the only job around, his employer will sense that in negotiations, and will have the upper hand.

Obviously it wouldn't be wise to quit without another job offer (or several) with an equal or better pay package lined up and ready to start.

Short of actually lining up those other job offers, being *willing* to walk away is not necessarily about quitting, but about knowing what your bottom line is.

Deciding ahead of time at what point your husband would start looking for a new position in earnest will keep him from feeling desperate and out of control of the negotiations.

If your husband is truly underpaid, and his employer can't or won't bring him up to the fair market rate, despite your best efforts, and it is keeping you from being a stay-at-home mom, then it is time for your team to move on to the next step—finding a better-paying job.

As Kenny Rogers would say, "You gotta know when to fold 'em."

REMAIN POSITIVE AND USE TEAM WORK TO MEET LIFE'S CHALLENGES

Treat life as an adventure. If you and your husband determine that he needs a new, better-paying position, look at it as an opportunity for which the outcome might be better than you had imagined.

A perfect example of this is Judy and her husband, Bob.

Bob was a dedicated employee. Always did his job. Never complained about the pay (much). He was the kind of guy who didn't like to change companies. Loyal to a fault.

Judy could not afford to be a stay-at-home mom with her five children and still pay the bills. In fact, they were having a terrible time of it.

Bob was making about $25,000 per year in the computer area. He had no formal computer certifications, although he had quite a bit of knowledge and experience.

After Judy did her homework, she knew that Bob was vastly underpaid.

Despite Bob's reluctance to make a change, Judy helped him to see that it was the best thing to do. She then prepared a resume, and posted his availability on the Internet on a site for technical professionals.

Bob received about 60 phone calls from that posting, and took a contract at $60 per hour, which equates to approximately $120,000 per year.

Bob has continued to receive contracts in the same pay range, and is now on contract to one of the Fortune 100 companies, who are so happy with him, they continue to renew his contract over and over. He has been there over two years now, and he *loves* working there.

If Bob had gotten a moderate raise, he might never have found out how much he could really earn, and he definitely wouldn't have found this new position where he is such a perfect fit.

If you and your husband determine it is time for him to move on, study the techniques in the following chapters on how to use Team Work to help your husband land a higher-paying job, apply them, and don't look back.

RESOURCES

Salary Surveys
www.salary.com
www.careerjournal.com
www.jobstar.org

Market Valuation for those earning $50,000 and over:
www.futurestep.com

Overtime Exemption Information

Department of Labor Wage and Hour Division
referral line
www.dol.gov
1-866-4USWAGE

SALARY WIZARD

A typical Product/Brand Manager working in metro Michigan—
Detroit is expected to earn a median base salary of $78,648. Half
of the people in this job are expected to earn between $67,888
and $90,283 (i.e., between the 25th and 75th percentiles). These
numbers are based on national averages adjusted by geographic
salary differentials. *(This data is as of June, 2001)*

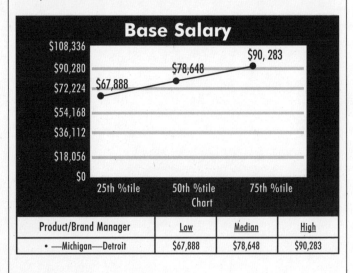

Base Salary

Product/Brand Manager	Low	Median	High
• —Michigan—Detroit	$67,888	$78,648	$90,283

Product/Brand Manager
Manages, develops, and implements product marketing activities
to maximize sales of an assigned product line. May require a
bachelor's degree and at least 4 years of experience in the field.
Relies on experience and judgment to plan and accomplish goals.
Typically reports to a senior manager.

Copyright 2000–2001 © Salary.com, Inc.

Sample Salary Survey

Chapter 5

Networking:
A Husband *and* Wife
Activity That Can Get
Your Husband a
Better-Paying Job

Sometimes it's not what you know, but who you know.

Networking is the art of developing your personal contacts, so that you have a network of friends and acquaintances that can help you **(and vice versa)** when needed.

Networking is NOT just about talking to recruiters and hiring managers, or asking your friends for jobs. Networking develops your **referrals to others, outside of your network, that you would like to meet.**

It is a lot easier for your husband to get in to see the CEO, or the branch or division manager, of a company he is interested in if someone he knows *also knows that executive* and is willing to let your husband use their name as a referral.

Your husband may even hear of a new, high-paying opportunity *before it ever becomes known to the general public,* if he has developed his network, and someone in it thinks of him when an opening becomes available.

Many high-paying opportunities can be found by networking, and you can help your husband to be an expert at it.

Networking for the Husband

Encourage your husband to make notes of people he meets who may be in a position to help advance his career.

Give him a "little black book" to keep these names and addresses in. If he is on the road when he meets someone who would be a good part of his network, he can keep their business card and write a quick note on the back of it with any important info about the person.

Potential candidates for his network would include:

- The people he does business with currently (clients and suppliers)
- Competition to his current line of work
- People in high positions in unrelated companies
- Recruiters and personnel managers

Joining trade associations is a great way for your husband to network. Your husband will get valuable information to help him in his current work while meeting others in his field, which may lead to the opportunity he is looking for.

Remind your husband to follow up with quick notes or short phone messages to the people in his network from time to time. When he runs across something he thinks may be of interest to someone in his network, like an interesting news item about their favorite hobby, he can clip it out and mail it to them. When something exciting happens in their life or work that he hears about, a quick note or phone message congratulating them would be in order.

Make sure your husband has some personal stationery on hand, as some men aren't used to writing letters outside of business.

You can also help your husband by clipping articles you run across that might interest someone in his network for him to pass on.

Networking for the Wife

It's not just who your husband knows, but who the *two of you* know.

That mom you just met at your daughter's Gymboree® class (who may be the wife of the manager of the company your husband would like to work for) could be the ticket to your husband's higher income.

Although knowing the wife of the CEO or manager is great, knowing *anyone* who works for your husband's target company can be an introduction to someone else in the company who is in a position to give your husband a better-paying job.

As a mother, you are in a position to meet quite a few people from all different walks of life. One of them may be able to help introduce your husband to the person who will hire him.

Think about who you meet in your daily travels. Does the wife of someone who works at your husband's dream company go to the same PTA meetings you do? Do you see them at the market? Are your boys in the same Scout Troop? Do they take their toddler to the same park you do?

Even if your contacts don't lead to a job opportunity for your husband, you will develop a larger circle of friends and acquaintances who will enrich your life and theirs just by knowing each other.

If you are currently working outside the home, while working out how to be a stay-at-home mom, keep in mind that your business contacts may be a good addition to your network that may lead to a new opportunity for your husband.

HERE IS A REAL-LIFE EXAMPLE OF TEAM WORK STYLE NETWORKING

Through her previous job, Amber got to know Linda, who was a hiring manager at another firm.

To help her husband, Paul, Amber called her

acquaintance one day and asked her *not for a job for Paul,* but if Linda knew of anyone who was paying well for Paul's particular skills.

Linda told Amber she would do some checking and get back to her. Linda did call back, and told Amber that although her company wasn't hiring for that at the moment, **someone in *Linda's* network was.**

Linda had made a call to her friend Rachel, who was the personnel director at a much larger company, who Linda knew needed someone like Paul, and gave Paul an introduction.

Paul was interviewed for the position at the larger company by Rachel and hired **at a 30% increase in pay from his current job.**

Paul was such an excellent fit with the new company that he was promoted twice in three years, and ended up at **more than double** what he was making at his previous job, and it all started with one phone call from Paul's wife.

That's Team Work!

In addition to the people you meet, another way you can help your husband to network is to keep up a Christmas or Holiday card list and include his network in it.

In today's rush-rush world, many families have stopped sending Christmas or Holiday cards, but it is an excellent way to stay in touch with family and friends while spreading cheer and reminding people of the joy of the season.

You might also consider a family newsletter once or

twice a year. On it put any highlights of your family's accomplishments that year. In addition to helping you keep up with family and friends, it is a way to keep your husband's network informed of his new raise or promotion, or of the new skill he learned by taking a night class.

If you are the social type, you may want to host parties or sponsor charity functions that give your husband a chance to connect on a social level with his contacts, while accomplishing something worthwhile for your community.

You could do this on your own, or get together with a couple of other wives you know to share the work. You could also join an existing group like a women's auxiliary, or even form your own if none exists in your area that seem appropriate.

NETWORKING IS ABOUT CONTACTS AND COMMUNICATION

It is a sad commentary on our world that neighbors sometimes go years without meeting each other. Neighbor helping neighbor is something we value when we see it, and something most of us would like to see more of.

Networking will help you bring about communication and give you contacts that you might not otherwise have known. Networking is not a short-term activ-

ity, done just when your husband is looking for a job—
it is a lifelong activity. You never know when your network contact might be in a position to help your team,
or when you might be in a position to help them.
Networking is a Team Work activity that benefits your
team and the world around it.

Resources

Recommended Additional Reading

*Rites of Passage at $100,000+: The Insider's Lifetime Guide
to Executive Job-Changing and Faster Career Progress*
by John Lucht

*The Five O'Clock Club Interviewing and Salary
Negotiation* by Kate Wendleton

SAMPLE NETWORK CHART FOR YOUR HUSBAND

Network Contacts

DATE	NAME	COMPANY	POSITION
6/14/01	Jim Smith	ABC Business	General Manager

E-MAIL	POSTAL ADDRESS	PHONE NO.
Jsmith@mail.com	1234 Main Ave. Anytown, USA	123-4567

Notes: Jim likes antique cars. Met him at the car show.

DATE	NAME	COMPANY	POSITION
7/25/01	Larry Smart	Big Corporation	Director of Sales

E-MAIL	POSTAL ADDRESS	PHONE NO.
Larry@bigcorp.com	1 Big Corp Drive Anytown, USA	555-4444

Notes: Met Larry at sales conference downtown. Likes our new products.

DATE	NAME	COMPANY	POSITION
8/14/01	Sam Taylor	Competitive Corp.	Marketing Director

E-MAIL	POSTAL ADDRESS	PHONE NO.
SamT@cc.com	2222 Right Road Anytown, USA	555-8888

Notes: Met at conference on new marketing ideas. His company is expanding and may need more marketing staff.

DATE	NAME	COMPANY	POSITION
11/17/01	Mary Gold	Best Personnel	Recruiter

E-MAIL	POSTAL ADDRESS	PHONE NO.
mgold@mail.com	8989 Busy Blvd. Nexttown, USA	555-7777

Notes: Helped Mary find a new sales manager. She said if I ever need a new job to call.

SAMPLE NETWORK CHART FOR YOU

Network Contacts

DATE	NAME	COMPANY	POSITION
06/25/01	Sally & Doug Southern	Hi-Tech Company	Stay-at-home mom (Sally) Company owner (Doug)

E-MAIL	POSTAL ADDRESS	PHONE NO.
sally@mommail.com	789 Nice Street Anytown, USA	555-2222

Notes: Sally's daughter Tiffany is in our Gymboree® class. Her husband, Doug, has a programming business downtown.

DATE	NAME	COMPANY	POSITION
8/24/01	Karen Matthews	Computer Sales Co.	Sales Mgr.

E-MAIL	POSTAL ADDRESS	PHONE NO.
KM@123mail.com	5555 7th Ave. Anytown, USA	555-0000

Notes: Met Karen at PTA. Nice woman with two sons, Matt & Greg, in 4th grade.

DATE	NAME	COMPANY	POSITION
09/17/01	Linda & Bill West	New Products, Inc.	VP Marketing (Bill) Stay-at-home mom (Linda)

E-MAIL	POSTAL ADDRESS	PHONE NO.
Lwest@earthmail.com	2222 Quiet Lane Anytown, USA	555-5555

Notes: Linda is on the same volunteer committee I am for American Literacy Campaign. She loves cats. Daughter Veronica is 3 years old.

DATE	NAME	COMPANY	POSITION
11/04/01	Richard North	Central Graphics	VP Sales

E-MAIL	POSTAL ADDRESS	PHONE NO.
Rnorth@cgraphics.com	5555 2nd St. Anytown, USA	555-1234

Notes: Worked with Richard on previous job. Helped him with the Anderson acct.

Chapter 6

Plan for Success

ARE YOU ON THE RIGHT PATH?

Having a good game plan can increase a team's likelihood of success.

Of course, an interesting and higher-paying opportunity you hadn't planned for may present itself—and it is fine to take advantage of it if it does. However, to ensure your success, your team should have a game plan that helps you achieve your goal.

Take the time to clearly define your objective, make sure it meets your financial needs, and find the best path to get there.

By doing these steps you may shorten the time it takes to accomplish your stay-at-home-mom goal.

HELP HIM FIND HIS PASSION

No, not in the bedroom—in the workplace! Does your husband really enjoy his work? Or does he make himself go, just to earn a living? Helping him find his passion can make his work more enjoyable for him and may lead to a higher income for your family.

What are his interests?

People tend to be much more enthusiastic about work if it relates to an area that really interests them. That enthusiasm can translate into more accomplishments, more promotions, and higher pay.

For example, if your husband is working as a bookkeeper, but spends his free time reading all the latest computer magazines and can't wait to tell you about the newest hi-tech developments, finding a way to work in the computer industry may unlock his passion.

Rather than switching fields completely, he may find a way to incorporate his interests with his experience. In the example of the bookkeeper, looking into a computer job in a financial services company would be a possibility.

The closer to his dream job the better, but in some circumstances you and he may need to get creative. Let's say he'd like to be a pro football player—his life revolves around sports—he knows every player and every score in recent history, but the reality is, he can't make the NFL. OK, how about a related job? Could he open a sports equipment shop? Create a football fanatic website and sell advertising to other enthusiasts?

What about a job working for a sports team in the marketing or financial department?

Talk to your husband one night after the kids are asleep. A good way to find his passion is to ask him to imagine he didn't need money and to describe three jobs he would like to do ***without being paid for them— just because they would be interesting.***

The funny thing about working for money alone is that it doesn't always lead to a lot of money. By ensuring that he enjoys his work or gets a sense of fulfillment from it, more of his creative energy will be applied to the job—and more resources for your family may come back from it.

WHAT ARE HIS DREAMS?

In addition to doing work that interests him personally, another part of finding his passion is thinking about what he wants to accomplish. It can be an accomplishment for himself, or what he wants to (or feels he can) give to the world.

In your private time with him, talk about what he would like to achieve. Does he want to entertain or inform people? Does he want to make life easier for others or help them in some way? Is there something in the world he'd like to improve?

He doesn't have to do it alone—remember, it often takes a team in the workplace to accomplish the end product. But even if it is in a small way, contributing to a larger goal can bring a tremendous amount of satisfaction.

Ask him if his current or prospective job offers him the chance to work towards what he wants to accomplish.

Sometimes it's just a matter of seeing how the job he has contributes to his goals, or recognizing the opportunities that are already there. By talking about the things that matter to your husband, the opportunity may be easier to hear when it knocks. Or, his goals may lead him down a different path that is more fruitful for him, and will bring out his passion and enthusiasm for his work.

Remember, you are a team. Do your best to encourage and support him in making his dreams into reality. If you can help him accomplish his goals, his success will have a positive effect on the whole family.

Even if his plans are for a ways off in the future, he will know that you share in his desires, and it will strengthen your team.

Making the Most of What You've Got

In addition to aligning your husband's work with his interests and goals, you will want to make sure that he will be paid well for his time and your team's efforts.

Finding out the potential income that different

jobs will bring your husband can help your team decide which of his skills to focus on in his resume, job search, or in starting up a new business.

Take the list of skills you made in Chapter 2, and do a search of positions that relate to them, and compare the salaries. What positions pay well enough to meet your needs? It's possible that the skill your husband considered a "side benefit" to his employer is really the thing that an employer would be willing to pay top-dollar for.

If he plans to be an independent contractor, you need to know the going rate for different specialties. And if your husband is considering becoming self-employed, establishing the potential want or demand for his service or product is an important first step in starting a business of his own. (More about that in later chapters.)

Do some checking on the potential income from areas that interest your husband if they are different from his previous experience and skill list. If the particular jobs that interest him won't meet your family's financial needs, try to find jobs that expand upon his interests or are related to them in some way, yet pay enough to accomplish your at-home-parenting goal.

You want to find out where the money is, and whether the job (or business) you are shooting for will meet your at-home parenting needs.

Look at where you want to end up, then work back from there to determine the best way to get there.

WHAT DOES IT *REALLY* PAY?

If your husband is considering training for an entirely new career path, you will want to investigate the expected financial results of his training before committing your time, energy, and possibly money to a particular course.

Don't buy a sales pitch, and **don't** rely on promotional materials provided by the training center. Do your own investigating.

For example, perhaps you and your husband have decided on finding him a job as a highly paid computer programmer. The local computer center is advertising their XYZ programming course as the best thing since sliced bread—sure to give you the career of your dreams! The course is affordable and fits your family's schedule. Do you jump at the "opportunity"? Definitely not.

Now is the time to do your research. You need to find out what kind of income your husband could reasonably expect to make as an XYZ programmer to determine if it would be enough to meet your family's needs.

The first step in doing that is to find out what those who are currently XYZ programmers are really making. Take a look at the salary surveys we discussed in Chapter 4. Also, check out the currently advertised positions for XYZ programmers and see what salary they are offering.

Additionally, talking to several recruiters or hiring managers can give you some really valuable information. Not only can they tell you the going rate for a particular skill, but they may be able to tell you about the current demand for that skill versus the supply of potential employees who possess that skill. Supply and demand can change, and being "ahead of the curve" may give your team an advantage.

A helpful recruiter or hiring manager may also let you in on information about which skills they see as hot, up-and-coming and highly marketable, and the pay range employees who possess those skills are commanding.

After getting unbiased information on the expected return on your investment, you will be in a better position to make a decision as to whether the XYZ programmer training is right for your team, or whether your husband would be better off pursuing another skill.

The Shortest Route

Your time is valuable, and every day you are not at the earning level you need to be home with your children is a lost opportunity for you and your family.

If your team's efforts lead to an unplanned opportunity that meets your needs—great! Go for it!

Meanwhile, however, make the most of your time and effort by having a game plan that includes your husband's interests, makes good use of his skills, and has a destination that will provide the income needed to make your stay-at-home-mom goal a reality.

Chapter 7

Marketing Your Husband

As anyone in marketing can tell you, a lot of the sale is about the packaging.

Think about how you shop. Something presented well, in an elegant way, and with its many virtues obvious at a glance, is much more likely to give you the feeling that it is a "good value," desirable, and worth having.

The same is true for resumes and cover letters. They are your husband's introduction to potential employers, and they create a first impression that can make the difference between getting an interview or being passed over without one.

Your husband may be a great manager, accountant, electrician, or supervisor, *but that doesn't necessarily make him good at marketing himself.*

Many men who are skilled in other ways do not know how to properly market themselves, and are therefore missing out on interesting and *higher-paying* opportunities they could be getting.

There is a technology, if you will, to writing an effective resume and cover letter that will get attention, present your husband in the best possible light, and most importantly, get him called in for an interview, which is the goal of a resume and cover letter.

This is something you can help your husband with as part of your Team Work approach to helping him get that better-paying job, so you can be a stay-at-home mom.

PROFESSIONAL RESUME HELP

There are many people who specialize in writing resumes—prices vary, and so do skill levels.

I've seen prices for resume writing services anywhere from $35 to $1,000 from what I consider the "Rolls-Royce of executive resume writing"—WSA Corporation. (More about their services in Chapter 8.)

You can locate a professional resume writer through your local phone book, or on the Internet. Resume.com (www.resume.com) is one site you can check, and there are many others.

If you are going to use a professional resume writer, ask to see some samples of their work.

Even if you are going to have someone else write

the resume, it is a good idea to know what should and shouldn't be in one, so you can let them know what you want, and have more control over the finished product.

DO-IT-YOURSELF RESUME TIPS

The list you made in Chapter 2 will come in handy in creating a new resume for your husband.

Some of the key points about creating an effective resume are:

1. **No typos.**

   While it may sound obvious, it is very important to proofread your husband's resume, as typos can create an image that is less than professional, and some (but not all) personnel managers report disqualifying otherwise attractive candidates due to typos. It is preferable to have someone other than the person who wrote the resume proofread it as well.

2. **Accomplishment-based information.**

   A resume is NOT a life story, it is a sales tool.

   Give potential employers more than just an accounting of the main duties or responsibilities your husband has had.

   Employers are interested in results. What they want to know is—***What can he do for them?***

Write about the accomplishments, not just the functions performed, and your husband's value will be made much more apparent.

For example, if your husband is in purchasing, instead of writing that he procured materials, write about the results of his work. Did he save the company money? Did he improve the company's cash flow by negotiating better terms with a supplier?

Think about what is important to the employer, and try to include those things in the resume and/or cover letter. Customer satisfaction? Profits—the bottom line? If you know where the focus of a particular employer is, you can tailor your resume and cover letter to let him know how your husband can help with his important issue.

3. **Quantify!**

Try to quantify achievements wherever possible. Giving specifics, such as dollar amounts, percentages, time frames, etc. will add credibility to your husband's claims and is likely to be more effective in interesting a potential employer.

"Reduced refunds by 30% in the first year," is much more specific than "reduced refunds," and "Closed 10 major clients adding $400,000 in revenue" is more convincing and gives the employer more to think with than "had high sales."

You should also avoid an excess of descriptive words like awesome, wonderful, incredible, etc. that may be perceived as bragging, and instead use quantified accomplishments to illustrate your husband's terrific qualities.

4. **Keep it simple.**

Employers are busy people, and like most of the rest of the world, they have grown accustomed to hearing news in "sound bites."

Your husband's resume has a few seconds to make an impact, or it may be passed over. The key points must stand out and communicate the advantages of hiring your husband in those few seconds.

A good Summary of Qualifications at the top of the resume can help with this.

Also make sure the entire resume is brief and to the point, while communicating the necessary information. An employer may get bored if the resume is too long, or the parts that are really important to him are buried in lots of unnecessary information, and may give up reading before he discovers what a great find your husband would be for his company.

5. **Put the focus on the positive.**

Emphasize the skills and experience that present your husband in the best possible way.

Use bold, italics, or "bullets" to show off key points quickly. Downplay any perceived "shortcomings."

For example, if your husband decided college wasn't for him after a semester or two and doesn't have a degree, just list the name of the college and the city and state, and write what he majored in, rather than write that he doesn't have a degree. If he didn't go to college at all, but has any professional certifications or took any non-collegiate training courses, list those instead.

Write more about the jobs that highlight his accomplishments or were more prestigious, and less about his entry-level positions.

Remember, it's your team's sales tool. While the information needs to be accurate, you can present it in a way that focuses on the positive information that you are trying to get across to the employer.

QUALITY COUNTS

Now that your husband has a great resume, make sure that it looks good too, and gives the impression that he is a "quality guy." Get some really nice paper, something in the fine business paper section of your local office supply store. A fairly thick paper, like 24 lb., made out of cotton or linen will look very impressive.

A good quality white paper looks sharp, and a light off-white can have a rich, elegant appearance. Some people like to use colored paper, but don't use any colors or prints that will distract from the resume or make it hard to read. Use color if you like, as long as it adds to the package, rather than detracts from it.

If you can, get a nice letterhead done for your husband, or use your laser printer to create one yourself. (If you don't have a printer, you can either write out his resume by hand, and then hire someone to do the typesetting or create it on their computer, or you can use the computer and printer at your local copy store for a few dollars an hour.)

A NOTE ABOUT COVER LETTERS

A cover letter has got to get the attention of the reader (your husband's potential employer) and inspire his interest, so that he will read the resume.

It also serves as an example of your husband's communication skills.

A cover letter follows similar rules to a resume:

- It needs to be brief and to the point.
- It needs to look professional.
- It needs to focus on the employer's needs, and how your husband can help him with those. (See example on page 69.)

THE VALUE OF MARKETING FOR YOUR TEAM

In the end it is really about how well your husband does the job, but without skilled marketing he may not get the chance to show the employer that he would be a great fit for that new, higher-paying job.

Marketing your husband correctly may be the step that is needed for your team to realize your desire to be a stay-at-home mom.

Time and money spent on marketing him may pay off handsomely in ways that are truly valuable to you, like a higher-paying job for your husband, and the freedom to stay at home full-time with your children.

RESOURCES

Resume Writing Service
www.resume.com

Additional Reading
The $100,000 Resume by Craig Rice

Rites of Passage and the companion *Executive Job Changing Workbook* by John Lucht

Building a Great Resume by Kate Wendleton

Winning Resumes by Robin Ryan

SAMPLE COVER LETTER

Bob Smith

1234 Main Street, Anytown, NY 56789
(123) 456-7890

David P. Richardson   March 14, 2001
Chief Executive Officer
Big Corporation
5555 Park Place
Anytown, NY 56789

Dear Mr. Richardson,

Could I help Big Corporation improve its bottom
line?

As supervisor of the XYZ Group at Large Company, I
increased sales in my area by 50% while reducing
expenses, which resulted in nearly double the profits
of the previous year.

Please contact me to discuss how I can help Big
Corporation get similar results.

Sincerely,

Bob Smith

Chapter 8

Finding the
High-Paying Jobs

High-paying jobs may seem elusive, but there are **lots** of them out there. The trick is knowing where to look.

Want ads can be deceiving. Most employment ads placed in the local paper are for the lower-paying jobs, and most of the higher-paying positions are not ever advertised.

So, how do you go about finding them?

THE FIRST STEP IS YOUR NETWORK

Many higher-level positions are filled by people who are already known to or are referred to an employer. In a position of trust, an employer will often prefer someone they know to a stranger, even if that person isn't the most qualified person they could find for the job.

Positions are also *created* for promising individuals who are introduced to employers, *where none existed before.*

Once your husband's skills are known to the employer, he may say, "You know, I was thinking of replacing that supervisor in ABC Department where production is so slow, but I hadn't gotten around to it. Maybe now that I know about Joe Smith, I'll do something about it."

Or, "Boy, our EFG Department is really doing great. I'd like to promote Steve to Vice President, but who could I get to replace him? Maybe Joe Smith could take over Steve's job so I can give him that promotion."

Or even, "I am so overwhelmed with business trying to run three companies. I wish I had a Chief Operating Officer, or an Executive Vice President. . . . Hey, that Joe Smith might be up to the job."

In the above three examples, positions were created and filled without ever being advertised, and it happens more often than you think.

By staying in touch with your network (and through other ways I will show you) your husband can be the "Joe Smith" that comes to mind when that employer thinks about creating and filling a new position.

Internet Job Listings

There are thousands and thousands of jobs listed on the Internet, and quite a few of them are not positions that would traditionally be found in the local want ads.

For example, there is a website called 6figurejobs.com (www.6figurejobs.com), and as you could probably tell, all the jobs listed on that site (and there are many of them) pay $100,000 per year and up.

Other sites have jobs at various pay rates—some lower, and some high enough that they generally won't show up in the newspaper.

Examples of these are www.vault.com, www.monster.com, www.headhunter.net, and www.employment911.com.

There are also industry specific sites, such as www.dice.com and www.itcareers.com for computer professionals, and www.jobs4hr.com and www.hrworld.com for human resource professionals. For construction employment there is www.tradejobsonline. Others can be found by putting your husband's industry along with the words "jobs" or "careers" into a search engine.

On many of the sites you can also post your husband's resume for potential employers as well as search for jobs.

Posting a resume is not as active as sending the resume to the specific employer that interests you, as you will be passively waiting for the employer to find your husband's resume, so you may not want to rely on this method alone.

Some sites help you send the resume you have posted on their site electronically to an employer who has listed a job opportunity with them, by clicking one button to automatically apply for that job.

On Dice.com your husband can also "announce availability" for a new job or contract, and put a sort of cover letter on the site with a message to potential employers and a listing of his technical skills.

Remember Judy in Chapter 4, whose underpaid husband, Bob, went from $25,000 per year to $120,000 per year? Dice.com was the website she used to announce Bob's availability and help him land that much higher-paying contract.

DIRECT MAIL IMPROVES THE ODDS

Direct mail can help your team find the jobs that are not advertised, and put your husband in the running for the ones that are.

Using direct mail puts your husband's resume in front of employers who are outside of your network of friends and acquaintances, that your husband does not have a personal introduction to.

Direct mail is mailing resumes and cover letters to prospective employers, **preferably in volume.**

It might only take a few letters, but then again it could take 1,000 or more. Many experts recommend a large volume to improve the odds of finding the employers that have a need for your husband's particular skills **at that exact time.**

Just like the direct mail that is sent to consumers to get them to buy a product or service, the result may be that just a small percent of the people mailed to respond, but even a small number of responses can lead to a great higher-paying job that your team might not otherwise have found.

When sending a resume and cover letter by the direct mail method, it is usually recommended to address it to someone two levels above the target job.

For example, if your husband is looking for a Vice President position, he would most likely send to the CEO. If he is looking for an accountant position, he should send to the person who supervises the head of accounting.

That person may contact your husband directly, and if not, when the resume is passed down to the next level in the organization from their boss, it will encourage them to call your husband in for an interview.

Always take the time to make sure that you have the correct name and title of the person you are sending the resume and cover letter to.

No "Dear Sir or Madam" or "To Whom It May Concern"

Taking the time to make sure the letter is addressed correctly will show a certain amount of interest in the company, and is much better manners.

There are many directories of companies at your local library. You may have become good friends with the reference librarian by now. (By the way, I have found most reference librarians to be wonderful people who seem to live to help people find information, and while I have sometimes been concerned that I was bothering them, I have always found that they didn't see it that way, but seemed instead to take personal satisfaction in the accomplishment of helping me find the information I was looking for.)

Some of the directories are divided by type of business or industry, others are by geographic area. Many will list the sales volume and number of employees so you can get a good idea of the size of the company, to see if it is one that your husband would be interested in.

The names of key executives are listed, but I strongly recommend calling to verify that the information is current, and that you have the correct spelling.

Directories get their information ahead of when they go to print, and the directory may have been on the shelf for a little while, too, even if it is the most current edition.

Make sure the person you are addressing the

resume to hasn't changed jobs, or you could waste your time, money, and effort.

Some directories also give short biographies on the key executives. The information in those may help your team. If your husband went to the same school as the employer, or was born in the same town, for example, that can be a conversation starter.

You can also research the company's website, and, in addition to executive bios, there will often be letters from the president of the company, or press articles quoting key executives, that may give you some insight into what issues are most important to them, and even what they are looking for in hiring new employees.

You could then tailor your husband's cover letter to show how he can help them with their key issues, or point out the attribute or skill your husband has that a particular employer is looking for.

A more generic cover letter that works for all employers by changing the address and salutation will save some time, but the extra effort to tailor the letter to a particular employer may improve the chance of a favorable response.

Either way, the important thing is that you do get a professional looking cover letter and resume mailed out, and the more the better.

Mailing out 1,000 or more letters is quite a task, and your husband may be very glad to have your help on it. In fact, you could invite some friends over and have a "mailing party," or hire a local teenager to help stuff the envelopes.

Professional Help with Direct Mail

If you are willing and able to spend the money, you can get professional help with your direct mail campaign.

For a fee, WSA Corporation will not only redo your husband's resume in their eye-catching style, but they will also do a full-scale direct mailing for him.

They maintain a large nationwide database of companies and their executives that they update regularly, and you can select companies from specific industries, specify a geographic area, or mail across the United States.

They will mail a large quantity of resumes and cover letters for your husband at one time. Their minimum order is for 500 letters, and they can send out many thousands if you choose.

They also offer a consulting service for interview assistance, to help your husband win that higher-paying job once he receives responses to his direct mail campaign, and to advise him on how to negotiate for the highest compensation possible, and which offers to take and which to pass on.

Your husband can receive a **free** resume critique and market valuation from WSA, to see what type of offers they think he would be likely to receive, by calling 1-800-WSA-CORP, or e-mailing them his resume at info@wsacorp.com.

Their services are fairly expensive, but if it leads to a job that is tens of thousands of dollars higher than your husband would find without using their services, then it would obviously be a good investment.

There are no guarantees, however, as to response rate to one of their mailings, so deciding whether or not to use them is a decision you and your husband should consider carefully before making the investment.

RECRUITERS AND THE "HIDDEN" JOBS

Many companies use professional recruiters to fill higher-paying positions, rather than advertising and trying to find the right candidate themselves.

If you plan to use a recruiter in your job search, you should know a little bit about them and how they work.

There are two kinds of recruiters. Both kinds are paid by the employer, which means that they are *working for the employer, not for the candidate.*

Contingency recruiters are recruiters who get paid only if they find a candidate that is hired by a company.

Contingency recruiters generally do advertise at least some of the positions they are trying to fill, and can be quite friendly and helpful in finding your husband a better-paying position.

They may have contacts in various companies *that are outside of your team's network,* and be able to give your husband the introduction that he needs to win an interview, and eventually a job, at his target company.

Keep in mind, however, that if your husband can

get in to the company directly, then there is no price tag on him that must be paid in order to hire him.

If the contingency recruiter sends him in, the recruiter may bill the employer as much as 30% of the employee's first year salary.

At a salary of $100,000 *it will cost that employer $30,000 more to hire your husband than it will for him to hire someone with similar qualifications that came to him without the help of a contingency recruiter.*

Therefore, if your husband can go direct, he should.

There is a trade off, though, where using a recruiter is the best choice, and that is when not enough opportunities are found without one. If your husband isn't getting enough interviews at the companies he would like to work for, then a recruiter getting him in is certainly better than waiting endlessly for the phone to ring.

You can find recruiters locally through the phone book, or nationally through a directory at the reference desk of your local library, but one of the fastest and most efficient ways I know of to reach a lot of recruiters who may know about the jobs you are looking for is Resume Zapper (www.resumezapper.com).

Resume Zapper electronically sends your husband's resume to hundreds or thousands (depending on the services you select) of recruiters at the same time.

You can select from a list of professions, and also geographic areas, if you want to send only to specific types of recruiters. The current charge for their service is $49.95, which is a lot less money than the postage would come to for a similar number of mailings, and a lot less work for you.

Although it would be helpful, you don't even have to own a computer to use their service. You can sign up for their service through the local library or copy center's computer. You will need to set up a free e-mail account for yourself, though, and check it regularly for responses. Two websites that offer free e-mail accounts are www.jobmail.net and www.mailcity.com.

If you don't have a computer at home, it would be best to specify that you prefer the recruiters contact you by phone rather than e-mail when selecting "preferred contact method" in the Resume Zapper sign-up form, but you will still need the e-mail account to sign up.

Not all recruiters accept resumes e-mailed to them through services like Resume Zapper, so if you don't get the response you are looking for using a service, don't give up. Just contact recruiters the "old fashioned way"—by phone or mail.

Personal contact can help, too, so it may be worthwhile for your husband to invest some time in meeting with and establishing a relationship with a particular recruiter, who may think of your husband *first* when looking for candidates for a terrific new position.

The Other Type of Recruiter Is the Retainer Recruiter

These recruiters also work for the employer on specific assignments, however, they get paid regardless of whether they find the employee, or whether the company finds the person themselves.

Part of what they are getting paid for is their expertise in conducting the search, and also in evaluating potential employees from any source. They are basically acting as consultants as well as trying to locate the right person for the job.

There is no added price tag for an employer hiring your husband through a retainer recruiter because of the type of contract they have with the employer. However, there is a whole other set of procedures to deal with when working with one, and it is not necessarily a fast process.

A lot of very senior positions are filled by retainer recruiters.

Generally they do not advertise the positions they are retained to fill, but look to candidates who they know are already working elsewhere, and would like an even better opportunity.

It is best to develop a relationship with retainer recruiters before you need a job.

Sending them a resume and cover letter is the first step, however, over time as your husband gets promotions, it is a good idea to write a short note to these recruiters to update his file.

It may take time for a retainer recruiter to contact your husband, and the first job presented may not be his dream job, but eventually these recruiters may offer him a chance at one of the choicest positions around.

Retainer recruiters can be located through the

phone book or local library. If it isn't clear by their listing which type of firm they are, just ask.

Retainer firms have certain rules that they are bound by that may make them seem less than eager to help a candidate.

For instance, if they have recently had a contract to place several people in a particular company, like Large Company, Inc., then they are bound for a certain period of time (usually two years) not to dismantle that company by trying to present any of Large Company's employees as potential candidates for a new client, **even if one of those people would be the best person for the job.**

If your husband happens to work for Large Company, and approaches the same firm that recently filled a position for them, he will not be presented to a potential employer even if he would be the perfect match and it is his "dream job."

Another practice that may make the retainer recruiter seem less than enthusiastic is that each recruiter in the office works on specific searches only, and if he doesn't have a current fit for your husband, there is no money for the recruiter to make there for the time being.

Retainer recruiters may or may not share your husband's information with the other recruiters in their offices at a particular time, but eventually they will release his file into the office database for another recruiter to pick up.

It may seem like the retainer recruiter isn't a fast

route to a great higher-paying job, but if you and your husband are willing to spend the time to develop the relationship, it may pay off with a referral to a fantastic position that he would not necessarily have found out about without knowing that recruiter.

While you might not want to rely on retainer recruiters to help with an immediate need for a higher-paying job, beginning to work with them now may lead to an even better position down the line that may come looking for your husband rather than the other way around.

Meanwhile, using the other resources in this chapter you can produce more immediate and still dramatic results in finding a higher-paying job for your husband.

Even if a recruiter helps your husband find a great higher-paying job right away, you should consider your relationships with both types of recruiters long-term relationships, rather than short-term ones.

A recruiter who enjoyed working with your husband (and received a nice commission on placing him at his new, higher-paying job) may come back to him in the future, when he gets a terrific new assignment at an even higher pay, or with a more ideal company, offering your husband his *next* position.

Through networking, direct mail, the Internet, and the two types of professional recruiters, you can gain access to an abundance of high-paying jobs, and increase your team's odds of success at finding a job for your husband that has a high enough pay for you to be a stay-at-home mom.

RESOURCES

Reference Books for Information on American Companies (Available at most libraries):

Thomas Register of American Manufacturers (annual)

Dun and Bradstreet Million Dollar Directory (annual)

Reference Book of Corporate Managements (annual)

Director of Corporate Affiliations (annual)

The Career Guide: Dun's Employment Opportunities Directory (annual)

Help Locating Executive Recruiters

The Directory of Executive Recruiters (annual)

Job Posting Sites

www.vault.com

www.monster.com

www.headhunter.net

www.employment911.com

www.6figurejobs.com

Computer Industry Jobs

www.dice.com

www.itcareers.com

Human Resource Jobs
www.jobs4hr.com
www.hrworld.com

Construction Trade Jobs
www.tradejobsonline.com

Resume Distribution Service
www.resumezapper.com

Executive Search/Resume Direct Mail and Consulting Service
www.wsacorp.com
1-800-WSA-CORP (1-800-972-2677)

Free E-Mail Accounts
www.jobmail.net
www.mailcity.com

Chapter 9

Getting the Job

Now that your husband has found those high-paying jobs, how does he turn those interviews into cash?

The answer is: Be prepared.

Using Team Work, you can help your husband to prepare for the interview. By helping him gather the information he needs, and practicing the interview with him, you can increase his odds of success in landing that new, higher-paying job.

Remember, a team that is well prepared has an advantage. After all, your husband's favorite football team or baseball team wouldn't go to a big game without practicing first—and neither should he.

Before the actual job interview, you and your husband can do your own "spring training," so that he can handle the interview like a pro.

Keep your sights on the goal: A job with the kind of salary that makes it possible for your family to afford at-home parenting. Being prepared could make all the difference in making that dream a reality.

INTERVIEW TECHNIQUES

There are many good books on interview techniques that you can pick up for your husband, but the following is an outline of some of the most helpful points.

1. **Make a good first impression.**

Appearances do count in interviewing. Unfortunately, some interviews are over before they start, due to poor grooming.

It is really a shame when a skilled, talented individual loses out on a good job (and the company loses out on the employee) because of something as superficial as appearance, but it does happen.

A clean body, (no dirty hair or fingernails) and a neat haircut (and no five o'clock shadow) are a good start.

No one likes to smell bad breath, so be sure your husband has some mints or chewing gum on hand for use right before the interview, even if he doesn't think he needs it. Better safe than sorry. (Obviously he should not chew gum during the interview, though!)

When it comes to cologne, it is better to skip it. A clean body smells OK by itself, and some people don't like or are allergic to fragrances. Your husband's interviewer may be included among them.

Clothing should be professional. Even in a traditionally casual field, like hi-tech, your husband should wear a suit and tie for the interview. Something conservative like navy blue is a safe bet. The suit should fit well, and be clean and pressed. A white shirt and a nice tie are recommended.

Once your husband has the job, he should wear whatever is appropriate for that office, whether it is a suit and tie, casual business wear, or jeans and a T-shirt.

Obviously, for certain trades a suit and tie would be so out of place as to make the interviewer wonder whether your husband really was skilled in that profession. However, even in that situation, a clean set of clothes or a crisp uniform give a more professional appearance, and will give the impression that your husband will take pride in his work, as well as his appearance.

2. **Be enthusiastic.**

Acting bored (or even worse—angry or apathetic) can hurt your husband's chances of landing the job. Interviewers usually want someone who will bring some enthusiasm to the job, and shows their enthusiasm in the interview.

Many otherwise qualified candidates have missed

out on jobs because they were not enthusiastic about the position during the interview.

David was up for a position as a senior executive for a hi-tech company. He went to the interview prepared and enthusiastic about what he could do for the employer. Some of the other candidates had more experience or technical skills than he did, but David got the job. The feedback from the recruiter was that the employer said David was the only candidate who really seemed enthusiastic about the job.

3. **Have a message.**

Rather than let the interview wander aimlessly, your husband should have a message prepared that "sells" him to the interviewer.

You can list our your husband's key skills and achievements in a way that can be communicated to the interviewer clearly and concisely (*preferably in one to two minutes tops*). Write them down on a card, and have him practice them over and over until he can rattle them off without difficulty.

These points comprise the main message that he will want to get across to the potential employer.

He will use them to answer questions like, "Tell me about yourself," or "What do you think makes you most qualified for this job?"

He should try to keep the interview focused on these points.

You can tailor these key points to match the needs

of a particular employer, once you know what their needs are.

Have specific examples he can give that *demonstrate each skill.*

Here are some examples:

"I am very good at marketing. The ad campaign I designed for Big Company had a 25% higher response rate than their previous campaign had."

"I can help with the bottom line. In my job at Mid-Size Corporation, I helped to streamline the production of the Widget Department, which cut costs by 10%, while still increasing production."

"I am skilled in programming in the 'C' computer language. Projects I have done for Big Company, Large Corporation, and Mid-Size Corporation were all completed on time, and they were very happy with my work."

4. **Do your homework.**

Your team should find out all you can about the company your husband is interviewing with. Use the Internet or your library to research the company. Try to get ahold of sales brochures or promotional materials from the company.

What is the focus of the company? What are their main products? Who is the competition? How is their product different or better?

Coming into the interview with this homework

done will make your husband a more attractive candidate, as it will demonstrate interest in the company and its products. It will also allow him to ask intelligent questions that will impress the interviewer and, at the same time, help your husband make sure that this is a company that he would like to work for.

For a large company, check out the executive bios that are available on most corporate websites or in directories at the library.

Often the executive bios or articles and press releases with executive interviews will give you insight into what is really important to a potential employer.

Your husband should ask for a complete written job description, if one exists, and become familiar with it.

In her book, *60 Seconds and You're Hired!*, career coach Robin Ryan suggests making a "Hiring Chart" with the employer's needs on one side and a brief description of the applicant's skill or experience that will fill that need on the other side. You or your husband may want to make that chart to show the prospective employer what a good match your husband would be for the company.

5. **Plan ahead how to answer tough questions.**
   Without planning, your husband may be caught off guard by the interviewer's questions and stumble around for an answer, or worse yet, ramble on and

on, losing the interviewer's interest, and possibly the job.

There are excellent books that give suggestions on how to answer the most common and difficult interview questions.

I highly recommend that you pick some up for your husband. After he reads them, you can help him practice answering interview questions until he feels confident and relaxed answering any of the questions in the books.

Examples of these are:

Q. **"Tell me about a mistake you made at a previous job."**

A. Your husband would be wise to give an example that doesn't work against him too much, such as: "In my first job as a junior account manager, I came up with an idea about how to reach a large number of prospects economically. I told my immediate supervisor, but he wasn't interested, and so I dropped the subject. Later, after that supervisor had been transferred, my idea was implemented, and it raised the department's sales by 20%. I learned that I should trust my instincts, and follow through to make sure I get my point across."

Q. **"Tell me about a boss you didn't like."**

A. Watch out, as the interviewer may be checking to see how easy your husband is to get along with, and whether there will be a lot of personality conflicts.

He would do well to answer that he has been fortunate to have worked with some very good people, and accomplished many things working under all of them, and try to steer the interview back to his message about his key accomplishments.

6. **Turn the tables—Ask questions.**

The questions that your husband asks may be more important to the outcome of the interview than the ones the interviewer asks him.

You can help your husband prepare for and practice this part of the interview as well.

A candidate who has done his homework and asks insightful questions about the company or its products will show his sincerity about his interest in the job, and that he is a person who stays on top of things.

Even asking basic questions about the job duties and the organization, such as "How many people will be reporting directly to me?" or "Can you describe the basic structure of your company?" will show that your husband is a thoughtful person and is interested in the company.

7. **Give the employer's needs top priority.**

Questions focusing on the employer's needs are very important. Your husband should ask about what difficulties or problems the employer is running into. Then he can point out how his skills or experience would make him qualified to help with those issues, and let the employer know that he is interested in doing so.

Even if the employer says that he isn't having any difficulties currently, focus on his needs by asking about what he would like to achieve.

What is his vision for the company? What would he like to accomplish in the next six months? What is the goal for the department your husband will be in (or running) for the next six-month period?

In addition to showing the employer that your husband can help him with his biggest concerns, these questions will show the employer that your husband wants the company to receive, not just give.

Important: Your husband should avoid asking questions about pay and benefits until after receiving the job offer. (*More on this in a later section.*)

8. **Be confident—Don't act needy or desperate for a job.**

While it is important to be enthusiastic about doing the job, a candidate should act confident in his abilities, and never seem desperate to just get any job.

Your husband needs to instill confidence in the interviewer that he has the skills they are looking for (or can learn them quickly), and that he can help the employer to accomplish his objectives. That confidence needs to start with him.

Rather than seeming pushy or aggressive, that confidence should be shown in a way that is reassuring to the interviewer that your husband will be able to do the job, and that the interviewer has made a good choice in asking your husband in for the interview.

Your husband should not discuss money problems, any difficulties in finding a new job, or the failure of his current employer to give him a raise after many years of service.

If he seems too needy, the employer may imagine there is some serious problem with his qualifications that is not readily visible and be leery of hiring him, even if he seems like the perfect candidate otherwise.

Remember that the interview process works both ways. Your husband is also interviewing them, to determine if this is really a company he will want to devote his forty or so hours a week to for the next so many years.

Your husband should keep in mind that although the company will pay him, he is helping the company by his efforts on their behalf, and by bringing his unique talent and experience to the job.

They will be lucky to get him, and you should remind him of that fact!

COMMUNICATION IS THE KEY

If your husband is nervous or uncomfortable talking to new people, or has difficulty getting people to understand him, or finds it hard to be a good listener, a communication course may be the ticket to helping him improve his interviewing results.

SALARY NEGOTIATION

Probably the most important thing for your husband to know about salary negotiation is to **wait until the job has been offered to him before trying to negotiate the pay.**

The reason for this is quite simple. When your husband begins interviewing, he and the employer are on opposite sides of the fence. Your husband is trying to overcome any barriers and "sell" the employer on the idea of hiring him.

Once the offer has been made, however, *your husband and the employer are on the same side.* They have the same objective—to have your husband take the job. And they will work together to overcome any barriers to that occurring.

Your husband will obviously have a much easier time negotiating from that point forward, as he will be negotiating with someone who already wants to hire him.

After finding someone he considers "the right man for the job," the employer will not be enthusiastic about continuing to spend his time and money on searching for another person to hire for that position.

Waiting until this point has the added benefit that

through your husband's successful interview technique of getting across his "message" about his key skills and experience, the employer now knows how valuable he really is, and may be willing to pay more than he had originally intended for the same position.

So, no matter how tempting it may be to ask about salary, bonus, vacation days, etc., before the job offer is made—don't. A little patience may be very rewarding.

It is a valuable, and sometimes overlooked, negotiating strategy to wait until after the job offer has been made.

What About Salary-Related Questions?

When asked about salary requirements early in the interview process, the best thing is to put it off by answering something along the lines of, "I am sure we will be able to come to an agreement on a fair compensation, but I would like to know more about the position first." Or, "Let's discuss that after we determine exactly what your needs are, and if I am the right person for the company."

If he is asked about his salary history, he may be able to avoid the issue for a while with: "I was in the market range for the position."

When he can no longer put the answer off, your husband should answer with the total compensation he received.

Compensation packages can include many things. In addition to base salary, any bonuses, stock options, benefits like employer contributions to 401(k) plans, scholarships for employees' children, etc., should be added into the total compensation figure.

The answer should also be given in a range, such as: "My compensation was in the $40,000 to $60,000 range, depending on bonuses." Or if he was underpaid, which he knows from the research you did for him, he should answer, "The market rate for a programmer with my background and experience is in the $70,000 to $80,000 range."

If he needs to tell the employer that he was paid $50,000 rather than a more appropriate $70,000, he should follow that information with something along the lines of, "I enjoyed working for the company, but with the amount of experience I have, I am no longer willing to make the trade off for the lower salary." It wouldn't hurt to have the salary survey to hand when negotiating salary issues.

When discussing salary requirements, it is always best to have the employer be the first one to mention a number, if possible.

That will give your husband the best position in negotiating for the salary he wants. Once the employer has offered the first number, then your husband can respond appropriately, depending on whether the offer is too low or is within an acceptable range.

A question from the employer about what your husband's salary requirements are can be met with a question *from* your husband such as: "What salary do you have in mind for the position?"

Negotiating the Offer

Once the job offer has been made, it is time to talk about the compensation.

The Acceptable Offer

If the base salary offer is acceptable, then your husband should respond with, "That amount would be acceptable. Let's go over some of the other details, too."

Compensation is a total package, and without negotiating some of those points, your husband could be leaving a lot of money on the table.

He should go over bonuses, medical and dental plans, paid employee training, 401(k)s, and any other employee benefits.

The Too-Low Offer

If the employer wants to give your husband the job, and he wants to take the job, but the initial base pay offer is too low, your husband should reply with something along the lines of: "I am very interested in working for the company, and I know I can help you with your needs, but I was thinking of a number in the x–x range."

Being willing to wait in the silence, and let the other person respond, is a useful part of negotiation.

If the offer is absurdly low, your husband can always laugh and reply with a number that is absurdly high, to relieve the tension. He would then proceed to come up with a more acceptable middle ground.

Keep in mind that hiring managers will sometimes

try to offer a number lower than they are really willing to pay, just to see what happens. It may actually be reassuring to them if your husband asks for more in that situation, as it will show them that he is confident in his skills and ability to do the job.

As we covered in the chapter on getting a raise, other parts of the package can be negotiated to make up for a lower base pay. This applies when negotiating compensation with a new company as well.

Paid medical for your whole family, a company car, bonuses, and other benefits can sometimes make up for the difference in the base pay your husband is looking for and the one that is offered.

Your husband should persist in negotiating, rather than being confrontational or walking away, as long as discussions are still occurring.

The negotiating process may take several conversations, just as the interview process may have.

NEGOTIATE THE JOB, NOT THE SALARY

If your husband runs into an impasse on the amount of the salary, he can negotiate the job duties and/or title into something that the employer *would* be willing to pay a higher salary for.

The employer may be willing to pay more for the position than he had planned to, if he sees that your husband will take on more responsibility than the original job description called for.

Also, your husband should keep in mind that he is interviewing with the company, not just for one position. They may have other openings later that *would* meet his salary needs, if this one doesn't work out, so he should be sure to leave a good impression.

THE OFFER LETTER

It is *vital* that you husband receive a **written** offer letter outlining the terms of employment. It should cover the **compensation** and also the **job duties.** The offer letter is your husband's protection.

The first way that the offer letter protects him is that it ensures that it really *is* a firm offer, before he gives notice at his current job.

The second way is that it makes sure that he really gets what was promised him in his new job.

A written offer letter helps to ensure that there are no misunderstandings as to what the compensation and job duties will be. Even with the best of intentions, misunderstandings can occur, and putting it in writing gives both parties a chance to make sure that they are in agreement on the important issues.

Also, people leave companies. If the person who negotiated with your husband made him promises that are not in writing, and they leave the company for any reason, he may not be able to get their replacement to honor the verbal agreements easily.

If an offer letter is not volunteered by the company, your husband must ask for one.

It should be done in a firm but pleasant way, such as: "I'm glad that we have come to an agreement. I am really looking forward to starting. If you can write me a note about the points we have discussed, then I can give notice to my current employer."

He can even offer to write down the agreements they have made, to ensure they are seeing eye to eye, and ask that they sign and date it to confirm their agreements.

File the offer letter away for safe-keeping.

It is your team's "insurance policy" of receiving the compensation needed to make it possible for you to be a stay-at-home mom.

RESOURCES

Interview Techniques and Sample Questions and Answers to Tough Interview Questions
60 Seconds and You're Hired! by Robin Ryan

Interviewing and Salary Negotiation by Kate Wendleton

Chapter 10

Continue to Grow

Congratulations! Your team scored!

You have successfully applied the techniques you've learned to help your husband get a raise or land that high-paying job that makes it possible for you to be a stay-at-home mom.

Team Work, however, doesn't end there.

It is equally important in helping you to be a stay-at-home mom that your husband keeps that new, higher-paying job, and continues to move up.

You can help with that.

Remember—Knowledge is Power.

Encourage your husband to continue to advance his education. The more skills he acquires, the more he can benefit his employer, and the more likely he is to succeed on the job, and earn a promotion.

He should inquire if his new employer has any training programs available to employees, or offers any assistance with the cost of outside training, as many companies do.

Many employers would be happy to know that an employee wants to improve his skills, and that they will likely be able to fill their next high-level vacancy with someone who already knows how things work at the company—namely your husband.

YOUR SUPPORT MAKES IT POSSIBLE

Along with the higher pay, your husband's new job may come with added responsibilities that occasionally require him to put in extra hours at work.

While it *is* important that your husband maintain a balance between work and family time, if he does have to work late or on the weekend *from time to time,* he will need to have your back-up and support.

Keep in mind that those extra hours are part of the job that is helping your family to have what is truly important to you—the freedom for you to be a stay-at-home mom.

The few extra hours that he may be away from home detract less from the overall quality of your life and the raising of your children, than the many, many hours you would be away if you were working full-time outside the home.

Your support and Team Work in caring for the family make it possible for him to do what is necessary to maintain his job and your family's newfound freedom.

Since continued training makes it easier to "work smarter" rather than "work harder," encourage your husband to add to his skills by advancing his education. It may help to lessen the frequency of the times he is away from home putting in extra hours at work.

If the situation becomes extreme, and it is adversely affecting your family, then you may need to search for a different job with equally high pay, and a less demanding schedule.

If you have gotten this far, you will know how to proceed using the Team Work techniques to make that a reality.

DON'T FORGET YOUR TEAM'S NETWORK

Sometimes companies go out of business, or lay off employees. To ensure your husband's continued employment at that new, higher pay rate, your team needs to do a little advance planning to prepare for any possible contingency.

Even if the company that your husband works for is very successful and stable, he may want to continue to move up the job ladder, either at that company or another one, to increase your family's financial comfort and security even further.

Maintaining your husband's network is a good step in that direction.

With your husband's new job (or raise at his old one) he will have the opportunity to add new contacts to his network. As important as that is, it is also crucial to maintain the contacts that he has.

That is something you can help with.

Keep up your Holiday cards or family newsletter. When you see an interesting article in the newspaper or a magazine that you know would be of interest to one of his contacts, clip it for your husband to send to his contact with a short note.

Pick out some nice personal stationery for him, and if he gets too busy, remind him every so often to use it to maintain his network.

If he wins an award, or has some great news to share, you can even help him make up an announcement letter or postcard that he can send out.

Continue to make contacts yourself that may help your husband's career.

In addition to the possibility of a future promotion or an even higher-paying job for your husband, you will be paid back handsomely for your time with a wider circle of friends and acquaintances that will enrich your life. And remember, a network is a two-way street. You may have the chance to help them, too, which is its own reward.

Doing the steps necessary to help your husband keep his new, higher-paying job, or move up to an even better one, should be a part of your team's game plan.

Chapter 11

Team Work for the Self-Employed Husband

What if your husband is self-employed, and wants to remain so, but his income is not sufficient for you to be a stay-at-home mom?

You can still use Team Work to help achieve your stay-at-home-mom goal.

In fact, if he has a very small business, or is a one-man company or contractor, he may really need your help, as he doesn't have a full team at work to help him succeed.

While the information on finding jobs won't work for him, many of the Team Work techniques will.

For example, you and your husband should still create the list of skills, experience, and attributes covered in Chapter 2.

It can help your husband by building his confidence, which may help him to close more sales or contracts for his business, and it will help him to identify key selling points he can use in getting new clients.

NETWORKING FOR THE SELF-EMPLOYED TEAM

The information on husband and wife networking applies to the self-employed team as well.

Networking will certainly help your husband if he is self-employed. It is something he can do to increase business now, while developing future business at the same time. You can get him a good book on the subject, or at least show him Chapter 5 in this one.

You can network, too, to help your husband improve his business income, at least until he has an effective sales force of his own that is helping him to maintain a high enough income without your efforts, for you to be a stay-at-home mom.

That mom at the Gymboree® class may be a potential client for your husband, or may know someone who could use his services or products.

And don't forget, you will benefit by expanding your circle of friends and acquaintances, just as the wife of the husband who is not self-employed will.

You may want to continue to network for your husband, even after he has a new, higher level of income. I'll bet many wives of successful self-employed men do.

Obtaining "Free" Publicity

Another way you can help him obtain leads, business contacts, and opportunities is to help him get free publicity.

With the right know-how, your work and creativity can get your husband the exposure he needs without breaking the bank for costly advertising.

If your husband has a local business, you can contact your local paper, radio, and TV stations. If your husband's business is regional, national, or international, you can expand your contacts to the media that cover larger markets as well. Don't ask them to do you a favor and write about your husband. Offer them what they need—an interesting story or event to write about.

For example, has your husband's business done an interesting project recently? Is there something unique about the work he does? Is a product or service he offers something people have questions about that he can answer? How about sponsoring some kind of contest or event?

In addition to the business editors, features or lifestyle editors may be a good source of publicity. Does your husband have a hobby that would make a good human interest story? If so, he might get coverage on that, which would, of course, mention what he does for a living or the name of his business as well.

If you like to write, you can learn how to send a press release, or if you are more comfortable calling, you can pitch your story idea on the phone. Even if you send written press releases, you will want to follow up by phone.

If you are shy and your husband is more outgoing, you can help him with ideas, how-to information, and researching contact info for local or other media, and he can make the contacts himself. If neither one of you wants to do it personally, another option would be to hire a public relations pro if his budget allows, or hire a college student who could write or make calls part-time.

The more contacts your husband makes, the more opportunities will come his way. You can take an active part in getting him known.

For information on working with the media, Joan Stewart, The Publicity Hound, has some useful tips on her website and in her free e-newsletter, which you can sign up for at www.publicityhound.com.

TRAINING IS THE KEY

If your husband's self-employed income is not where you and he need it to be, training is the key to improving that income.

You can help your husband by getting him books on promotion and marketing for small businesses, and business management.

There are many books out there about how to promote without spending a lot of money, that he may find useful. A couple of examples of these are *Guerrilla*

Marketing and *Guerrilla Advertising* by Jay Conrad Levinson.

Or you can help him to find the training that is right for him.

The courses from the American Management Association are relatively fast and inexpensive, but they could open the door to a much higher income for your husband.

Does he need help with increasing sales? Budgeting and managing expenses? How to develop new markets for his products and services? There are courses that can give him the tools to create the higher income that your family needs for you to be a stay-at-home mom.

In addition, if he is a contractor, adding to his skills by training may help him to earn a higher hourly rate. You can help him to find out which training courses would add to his value as a contractor that are within your budget and schedule. The list of resources in Chapter 3 may help you with this.

Of course, for him to train, he will need your back-up and support as well.

BEEN THERE, DONE THAT—USING AN EXPERIENCED CONSULTANT CAN IMPROVE YOUR HUSBAND'S ODDS OF SUCCESS

If he is in business for himself, you can help your husband locate a management consultant who is knowledgeable in your husband's field and can, for a fee, conduct an analysis of your husband's business and make recommendations as to the changes that will produce the most drastic improvement in his business.

An experienced guide or mentor can make the process much easier for your husband to realize the type of income that he probably had in mind when he decided to go into business for himself.

In many fields there are people who have already run very profitable businesses. Rather than re-invent the wheel, it makes sense to profit from their experience.

Trade associations for your husband's line of work can be a good source of advice through their seminars, roundtable discussion groups, book offerings, or courses. Some trade associations will help their members to connect with others who have had a lot of experience, have been successful in their field, and have offered to act as mentors to interested parties.

Locating and taking advantage of consulting and/or training that improves the "bottom line" (profits) of your husband's company, and makes it possible for you to be a stay-at-home mom, is time and money well spent.

Also, money paid for course fees and/or hiring a management consultant can generally be written off by business owners. Check with your tax professional for details.

These are just some of the ways you can use Team Work to help your husband if he is self-employed. You may be able to come up with a lot more.

The idea is not for you to go to work full-time at his company though, as that would defeat the purpose.

You can help him, however, using the Team Work techniques (such as building confidence, networking, helping him to train, etc.) while being a stay-at-home mom.

Whether your husband works for a company, has his own business, or is a self-employed contractor, using Team Work can help your team achieve its stay-at-home-mom goal.

RESOURCES

Books
Guerrilla Marketing by Jay Conrad Levinson

Guerrilla Advertising by Jay Conrad Levinson

101 Ways to Promote Your Website by Susan Sweeney

Information on Getting Free Publicity
Joan Stewart, The Publicity Hound
www.publicityhound.com
1-262-284-7451

Management Training
American Management Association
www.amanet.org
1-800-262-9699

Trade Associations
Consult your local phone book, but for additional help: www.associationcentral.com

Reference Books
Encyclopedia of Associations: National Organizations of the U.S. (available at most libraries)

National Trade and Professional Associations of the U.S. 2000 (available at most libraries)

Management Consultant Referral Service
The Consulting Exchange
www.cx.com
1-800-824-4828

Chapter 12

Alternative Income Sources—How to Earn Extra Income

In *How to Help Your Husband,* I have purposely focused on techniques that can help your husband to earn more money at his primary job.

The reason for this is that I feel that it is important to have a balance in life between one's work and the rest of life.

Personal growth, family life, social causes, and spiritual matters are all important parts of life, too, and their neglect not only affects those areas, but will eventually impact on one's work as well.

I also believe that ideally, one's primary job should pay enough to support a family, and that armed with the knowledge in *How to Help Your Husband,* it is something that can be achieved by all, and that working for extra income should provide just that—*extra* income.

That being said, there are times when putting in extra hours to make more money can be a viable alternative, at least *for the short-term.*

An example of this would be a situation where a family could get by on the husband's current income alone, if a particular bill or debt was paid off fairly rapidly by some short-term extra work hours.

Or when those extra work hours lead to a new, higher-paying job or career.

Or to build a "nest egg" or provide additional security for the family by not being dependent on only one source of income.

Remember, though, it is important to have a life, too, not just spend life trying to make money!

OVERTIME

Probably the simplest and most obvious alternative income source is for your husband to arrange to work some overtime hours at his current job, if that is a possibility.

Keep in mind that the time you spend alone with your children while your husband puts in some short-term overtime hours will probably be less disruptive to your family than if you went to work full-time outside the home to make the extra money.

If there are no opportunities for overtime hours on your husband's current position, there may be other areas within the same company that have a backlog which he could volunteer to help his employer handle.

Again, for the long-term, it would be better for your husband to spend the extra hours learning a new skill, networking, contacting prospective employers, or otherwise advancing his career, rather than endlessly putting in overtime hours and maintaining the same rate of pay that is causing him to need to work overtime to meet his financial goals.

A SECOND INCOME—THE PART-TIME JOB

The same theory that holds true for overtime holds true for working at a second job, with the exception of when the second job *gives your husband skills or experience that helps him to earn more money at his primary job.*

For example, if your husband is good with and interested in computers, but cannot afford to leave his current job to take an entry-level position full-time, a part-time job in that field could help him to make a smooth transition to a high-paying career. (Although some of the entry-level positions in the computer field pay more than many other full-time jobs, so in the case of the computer field, that may not be an issue!)

Another example would be where your husband's skills in an area are of a beginning nature, and the part-time job provided the opportunity to learn on the job, in almost a paid internship type of position.

Of course, if he is very skilled and experienced in

his primary line of work, he may want to pursue a part-time opportunity in the same field, where he is likely to be very much in demand.

Remember the list of skills you and your husband made in Chapter 2? Some of those skills may be useful in establishing another source of income.

Temporary employment agencies that handle overloads and backlogs can be a good source of information about companies that could use your husband's talents on a part-time basis for a while.

Guru.com (www.guru.com) is a website that lists contract opportunities for freelance work. Some are full-time, but others are part-time, and some can be done from home.

Your husband should keep in mind that if he does go to work for another company part-time, it is an excellent opportunity to network, as he will meet new people in the industry he is interested in who may be able to help him in the future (and vice versa).

Also, if he does an excellent job for them part-time, they may offer him a new, higher-paying full-time position on the spot.

It is important for your husband to know what the policy of his current employer is in relation to employees having second jobs, or working for any competitors, so that he does not do anything that would jeopardize his primary source of income without having a firm written offer for another full-time position in hand.

WORKING FOR HIMSELF

People will pay for your husband's knowledge and skills.

Another alternative source of income is for your husband to find people who will pay for his knowledge and skills as an independent consultant or tutor.

Does your husband work as a bookkeeper during the day? He could offer to help individuals or small businesses straighten out their records or devise a bookkeeping system for them evenings or weekends.

Is your husband an expert on model trains? He can offer to give a class on model trains at the local community college on weekends. Does he have a green thumb? He could offer a class or private consultation through several local nurseries. A hobby can lead to an enjoyable source of additional income.

If your husband is good with basic computer skills, he could offer to be a "Computer Tutor" for first-time computer purchasers who would love to have some one-on-one help setting up their computer or learning the basics of how to use the computer, or access the Internet, in their own home.

A local computer store might be happy to sponsor your husband by giving out his business card or flyer, since it could help them to close a sale if their customer is unsure of whether they will actually be able to *use* the computer once they get it home!

Distributing flyers to senior citizens' centers offering them a special discount might be a good way to get clients, while helping seniors to gain access to health and other information, and to be able to e-mail their family and friends.

You and your husband could also promote and market that service many other ways on a shoestring.

Books such as *Guerilla Marketing* and *Guerrilla Advertising* by Jay Conrad Levinson and many others can give you tips on how to promote without investing a lot of money.

Have you ever said to your husband: "You could write a book on [fill in the blank]"?

If he has a great deal of knowledge in an area, whether from work, a hobby or general interest, or through life experience, he *could* actually write a book or booklet that he could sell either through a publisher, or he can self-publish once he learns how.

Two good books on the subject are: *The Self-Publishing Manual* by Dan Poynter and *1001 Ways to Market Your Books* by John Kremer. *The Writers Market* (annual) can give him information on how to sell books or booklets to publishers, and lists hundreds of publishers who buy written works with contact information and the type of material they are looking for.

If he has knowledge to write a book or booklet about, but isn't into writing, he could hire a ghost writer (someone who would write down his ideas for him) to get the book or booklet done.

In addition to mainstream book sales to a general

audience, if your husband is expert in, or has useful information for a particular field—such as hiking or soccer playing, he can market his book or booklet to a specialty market like sporting goods stores or sports groups.

A booklet on model trains would probably do well through collectors' clubs or model train stores.

A booklet doesn't necessarily take a long time to write, and can be produced fairly inexpensively.

You or he could "test the waters" to see if there is a market for the booklet by checking with some likely purchasers or sales outlets to see if they would be interested in such a booklet, if he were to write it.

OTHER BUSINESS IDEAS

If your husband would like to go into business for himself, there are many products and services that he could provide.

A successful part-time business can even turn into a full-time income that exceeds your husband's salary and eventually replaces his day job.

However, I do NOT recommend borrowing large sums of money to start up a business.

If you borrow a lot of money to start a business, and the business doesn't succeed, then it will be even more difficult to realize your team's stay-at-home-mom goal with the new debt added to your financial obligations.

When starting a new business, it is important to keep your team's goal in mind.

There are many businesses that can be started without spending a lot of money. If your husband decides to go into business for himself, it would be wise to start on a shoestring, and build from there as the business grows.

If your husband is interested, you can pick up books on the subject for him, such as: *Success For Less: 100 Low-Cost Businesses You Can Start Today* by Bob and Terry Adams, or *77 No Talent, No Experience and (Almost) No Cost Businesses You Can Start Today!* by Kelly Reno, and the *Guerrilla Marketing* and *Guerrilla Advertising* books by Jay Conrad Levinson mentioned earlier, or any number of other books on the subject.

Once your husband is in business for himself (or before he goes into business), training in successfully running a business and in the specific field that his business is in will increase his odds of success. The American Management Association, your local community college or the trade association that is appropriate for your husband's business are good places to look for such training.

Even if he is only in business for himself part-time, the chapter on self-employed husbands now applies to your husband as well.

AN ON-LINE BUSINESS

A website on the Internet can provide a fairly inexpensive way to start a part-time business.

There are many ideas for on-line businesses that can be run from home. You can help your husband come up with an idea for an on-line business that he would enjoy by going over his list of skills with him, as well as his interests and goals.

You can also pick up books for him with ideas for on-line businesses that might appeal to him or help to inspire him to come up with an idea for an on-line business of his own.

121 Internet Businesses You Can Start From Home by Ron E. Gielgun is one example.

For very little money, a website can be up and running that can promote your husband's service or product.

Registering a unique name for your husband's website can be done for about $15 at www.123domains.com, and for various prices at other registration sites.

Your husband will need a hosting company for his website. A hosting company is the place that stores his website and processes the communication between Internet users and his website. The hosting company also makes it possible to do business on the Internet (e-commerce) by taking orders from customers on-line once your husband has a merchant account set up to process credit card transactions.

There are many hosting companies available for website owners. Value Web (www.valueweb.net) offers a very complete service at a very competitive price. Their current charge for an e-commerce site is about $50 per month.

If your husband plans to have his business take orders directly on the Internet, he will need to set up a merchant account so that he can accept payments by credit card. Merchants accounts for home-based mail order and Internet businesses have become much easier to get in recent years, and prices vary considerably among providers. Value Web has links to information on a merchant account provider on their website, or you can shop around and find the one that you like the best or that offers the best price and terms.

According to their website, Value Web's e-commerce package actually comes with free software that helps you to build your Internet site, and that is designed to be used by non-programmers so that a novice computer user should be able to follow the instructions and get their site up and running.

For a fee, your husband can hire a professional website designer. Professional website design runs anywhere from about $300 up to many thousands. My experience has been that the price does not always reflect the quality, but is rather whatever the designer thinks they can charge. I have seen some sample work from lower-priced web designers that I thought was superior to the sample work of a designer that quoted me a price around ten times higher than theirs.

When using professional website designers, ask for several sample sites you can visit, and *check around for a price you can afford.* The site needs to be aesthetic, and easy to use, but you can always make improvements to a site once it is up and bringing in income.

In addition to e-commerce sites that actually sell products or services on-line, there are sites that are really just advertisements for a company's product or service. Those sites provide information, and refer visitors to a phone number or address where they can obtain the product or service, but don't actually take orders on-line. The cost to host a site like that is smaller, usually around $20 per month, and a merchant account is not necessary, although it may be helpful for processing credit card orders off-line.

Content-only sites (sites that provide information rather than advertise or sell the site owners' products or services) can be profitable as well by selling advertising space to businesses that tie in to the type of information offered on the site.

A good example of this is Askthebuilder.com (www.askthebuilder.com). This construction information site has earned a six-figure income for its owner through sales of advertising space on his site alone.

The book *Striking It Rich.com: Profiles of 23 Incredibly Successful Websites You've Probably Never Heard Of* gives inspiring and interesting inside information on the "Ask the Builder" site, and 22 others.

In addition to seeking out appropriate advertisers to pay for space on your husband's site, a "turn-key" banner program may help create an income stream quickly and easily.

Sites like www.commissionjunction.com list companies that will provide a small banner ad, which is ready to go and easily placed on your husband's site. In exchange for placement, they will pay you a commission on all sales that result from one of your visitors clicking on the banner and making a purchase at the advertiser's site.

I know of one person with a "home-grown" site who received over $1,000 per month from one of his commission junction banner ads alone.

Of course, sites like Amazon.com also have commission or affiliate programs, but a banner broker like commissionjunction gives you many banner choices, and allows you to monitor the effectiveness of the banner ad regularly and make changes if you aren't happy with the response of a particular banner.

While your husband may or may not get rich starting a business on the Internet, it is definitely possible to earn an additional part-time income from an on-line business, or to use a website to promote an off-line business and add to its income.

As with any business, however, there are no guarantees of income with an Internet-based business, so you and your husband should do your research, and decide carefully whether you want to spend your time, energy and money on starting up a business before proceeding to do so.

Making the Most of the Internet

There are many businesses on-line and off that can benefit from the Internet. Even if your husband prefers an off-line business, he may want to use the Internet as a source of advertising for his off-line business.

Whether your husband's website sells a product or service on-line, advertises for his product or service, or is a content-only site, *increasing traffic to his website is a key part of running a successful Internet business.*

In order to get advertisers, it will help to maximize the traffic to your husband's website so that the potential advertisers will be gaining more exposure for their businesses.

And, of course, customers cannot buy your husband's product or service from his website if they never see it.

101 Ways to Promote Your Website by Susan Sweeney is a very good book about the Internet and how to get visitors to your website.

Promoting a website correctly, and getting it a top listing in the search engines that help Internet users to locate sites, can make all the difference between having a thriving on-line business, and wondering whether anyone is really out there in cyberspace.

Many promotional actions for Internet-based businesses can be done with little or no cash outlay, such as trading links to your site with related, but not competing websites for links to their sites.

In addition to helping your husband find out how to get traffic to his website, you can also help your husband promote his website by giving out business cards with his website on them, and going on the Internet to appropriate chat rooms or newsgroups and mentioning his site as a form of on-line networking for your husband.

Advantages of the Internet

A virtual business run on the Internet and operated from home avoids many of the costs associated with a "brick and mortar" business, such as rent and utilities for office or storefront space.

A home-based Internet business also has the advantage that even though your husband will be working, he will be home with you and your children.

With a completely on-line business, your husband can even set his own hours to be compatible with your family's schedule (like after the children are asleep, or after your daughter's piano recital, for example,) since the Internet is running 24 hours a day.

And the Internet will allow your husband to reach clients locally and from many parts of the world that would normally be much more expensive and difficult to reach.

EARN EXTRA MONEY AND STILL HAVE A LIFE

With the Internet, traditional off-line businesses, overtime, part-time jobs, freelance work, getting paid for knowledge and skills by consulting, writing, or tutoring, there are many ways for your husband to earn extra money.

Ideally, however, through your team's efforts, your husband will be able to make enough money at his primary job or business for you to be a stay-at-home mom, while having time for all the other important parts of life, like personal, family, social, and spiritual matters.

Therefore, if your husband does put in additional work hours to earn extra money, it would be best to choose a method of earning extra money that would lead to a much higher income at his primary job or business, if possible.

If a continuing second income is desired, it is important to arrange things so that there is a balance in your team's life between making money and living the life that you have worked to achieve.

Having a balanced life will help your husband to succeed, as he will be able to bring more to the job when he is working by being rested and refreshed than if he is tired and burnt out from working 24 hours a day.

Also, by spending time on family, social, and spiritual matters, his motivation and creativity are enhanced and he is enriched personally, which can make it easier for him to accomplish his financial goals for his work or business.

By selecting a way of making extra money that leads to a higher income at his primary job, or arranging an alternative income source that aligns with your family's needs and allows time for other interests, or by simply helping your husband to earn more money at his primary job, you can use Team Work to help your husband make more money so you can be a stay-at-home mom, and still have a life.

RESOURCES

Additional Reading

Success For Less: 100 Low-Cost Businesses You Can Start Today by Bob and Terry Adams

77 No Talent, No Experience and (Almost) No Cost Businesses You Can Start Today! by Kelly Reno

Guerrilla Marketing by Jay Conrad Levinson

Guerrilla Advertising by Jay Conrad Levinson

Striking It Rich.com: Profiles of 23 Incredibly Successful Websites You've Probably Never Heard Of by Jacyln Easton

121 Internet Businesses You Can Start From Home by Ron E. Gielgun

101 Ways to Promote Your Web Site by Susan Sweeney

The Self-Publishing Manual by Dan Poynter

1001 Ways to Market Your Books by John Kremer

Reference Book (Available at most bookstores and libraries)
The Writer's Market (annual)

Contract Assignments
www.guru.com

Website Name Registration
www.123domains.com

Website Hosting
www.valueweb.net

Chapter 13

About the Future

HELPING SOCIETY VALUE THE STAY-AT-HOME MOM

By helping society to value the stay-at-home mom, you will not only be helping your team to achieve its stay-at-home-mom goal, you will also be making it easier for future generations to achieve their goals as well.

A stay-at-home mom is a valuable and important member of society.

Her contribution to society should not be underestimated.

Our children are the future citizens whose votes will determine the kind of country America will be.

They are the future scientists, political leaders, artists, and educators who will change the world.

What about the contribution of raising a child who, because of the love and support of his stay-at-home mom, has the confidence, value system, and educational strength to find the cure for cancer, or invent something that improves the quality of life for the entire world, as Thomas Edison did?

If it wasn't for Edison's mother homeschooling him when the educational system of the day gave up on him, we might still be using oil lanterns to see at night.

Today we have a situation like Edison had, but in enormous proportions. The fraudulent labeling of children as having "ADD" or "Attention Deficit Disorder," leading to the widespread drugging of children, has even been extended to toddlers now.

This is a national shame.

Rather than deal with the issues behind "learning problems" we as a nation are too busy to handle, we have accepted psychiatry's "quick fix" of drugging children into submission, creating a new generation of drug addicts whose minds and bodies are ravaged by these stimulants before they have a chance to reach their potential.*

The increase in violence among children, the increase in street and "behavioral" drug use, and the lack of literacy and other educational shortcomings that are prevalent, are warning signs about our soci-

---

*Source: Dr. Fred Baughman, pediatric neurologist. "The Future of Mental Health: Radical changes ahead." *USA Today* magazine, March 1997. "Ritalin for Infants and Toddlers c/o Uncle Sam." *USA Today* magazine, January 1999.

ety's lack of attention to the importance of raising the next generation.

While having more moms choose to stay at home with their children will not fix all the ills of society, in my opinion it is a step in the right direction.

It is a very short-sighted society indeed that does not see the value of its children and their mothers.

Many of the freedoms women now enjoy have been hard won. The right to vote, to own property, and to be paid fairly are major improvements to the lives our ancestors lived, and should not be taken for granted.

However, while freedom is a desirable goal, is it really freedom to be *obligated* to give up your desire to raise your children as a stay-at-home mom to bear the financial responsibility of the family?

Freedom means choice. The choice to stay at home with your children is a freedom that many women would like to have. The women making that choice should be applauded for their integrity in living their lives in the way they feel is best, and for their contributions to their families and to society.

The new millennium is the time to bring about a new idea in society. One that looks at the big picture. One that restores the family unit and family values, recognizes the importance of the family, and makes it fashionable to raise the next generation as a stay-at-home mom.

Americans for Family Values, or a similarly titled group, could be a vital force in forming a society that values the stay-at-home mom as she so rightly deserves, through lobbying for legislation, sharing of resources, public relations, support, and education for families, and those who influence them.

Whether alone or as part of a group, you can help society to value the stay-at-home mom, if only by proudly communicating your choice when asked "What do you do?"

Society evolves through ideas. Your ideas and your opinions do matter.

WHOSE KIDS ARE THEY ANYWAY?

The government cannot do as good a job of raising children as their parents can.

It is up to the parents to teach their children lessons of character, moral values, and beliefs in a loving family environment.

Government, in its ever increasing complexity (think IRS codes), has consistently focused on providing more and more government sponsored child-care programs for households where both parents work outside the home full-time.

These involve, of course, more and more spending and more and more use of resources (staff, materials, buildings, etc.) in a misguided attempt to solve the problem.

Then follow other programs to deal with the increasing violence and drug use of "at-risk" kids with less parental supervision than needed.

Of course, according to the government, we also need more programs to deal with our educational crisis, since parents are not available after school to help children with their homework, and are not home in the early years to ensure a good academic foundation for their children.

These programs come with even more spending, and the need for even more resources, such as staff, materials, buildings, etc., and therefore even higher taxes for American families, to support all of these government programs.

Let's take it back to a simplicity for a moment. What is the problem that the government is trying to solve?

The problem is that many families cannot afford to have the mom stay at home to raise their children.

Instead of adding more and more complex "solutions" to the problem, that then themselves need solutions, **let's eliminate the problem.**

Let's make it easier for families to afford to have the mother be a stay-at-home mom.

A simple way to do this would be to initiate a tax break by way of an *entirely lower taxation rate* for "Head of Household with a Stay-at-Home Mom."

A significant tax break would make the difference in many families between the mother needing to work outside the home and being able to be a stay-at-home mom.

Since many families would prefer to have the mother stay at home with the children if they could afford to, it is easy to see that addressing the *actual* situation, *by making it easier financially for families to have the mother be a stay-at-home mom,* would reduce the need for so much government intervention in our lives and reduce the amount of government spending, making it easier to provide this much-needed tax break for families.

The job of government is not to replace the family, but to support and defend it.

You can do your part by supporting legislation that would bring this about.

Get involved. Write letters to your Congressmen—Vote. It's *your* country.

After all, that would be the "Team Work" approach to society.

RESOURCES

To Locate and/or Write to Your Congressmen
www.congress.org

More Information on ADD/ADHD Fraud
www.adhdfraud.org
www.ritalinfraud.com

Sites of Interest to Stay-at-Home Moms
(or would-be stay-at-home moms)
www.athomemothers.com
www.stayathomemom.com
www.momsonline.com
www.momsclub.org
www.homebodies.org
www.mainstreetmom.com

Organizations of Interest to Stay-at-Home Moms
International Moms Club
(over 1,200 chapters)
www.momsclub.org
25371 Rye Canyon
Valencia, CA 91355

National Association of At-Home Mothers
www.athomemothers.com
406 East Buchanan Avenue
Fairfield, IA 52556

Conclusion

I hope that you have found some of the techniques in *How to Help Your Husband* interesting and useful.

Only you and your husband can decide which techniques are right for your team.

The Team Work concept, however, is universal.

By *working together,* doing the research for their particular situation, and acting on the necessary steps, any couple can raise their income, and accomplish their stay-at-home-mom goals.

Be persistent in doing what it takes. The prize is certainly worth the effort.

The benefit to your family will be enormous, and while being a stay-at-home mom has its challenges, too, the joy and sense of fulfillment you will receive are priceless.

I wish you all the success and happiness that Team Work and being a stay-at-home mom can bring.

I would love to hear from you with your stories of success in applying the Team Work concept and the techniques in this book. Feel free to write to me at the address below.

Good luck and God bless!

Joanne Watson

Warner Books
Attention: Author Mail
1271 Avenue of the Americas
New York, NY 10020
e-mail: authors@myfamilybooks.com

Resources

Bibliography

Additional Reading

Getting a College Degree Fast by Joanne Aber, Ph.D.

Distance Degrees by Mark Wilson, M.A.

How to Earn a College Degree Without Going to College by James P. Duffy

60 Seconds & You're Hired! by Robin Ryan

Interviewing and Salary Negotiation by Kate Wendleton

Rites of Passage at $100,000+ by John Lucht

Executive Job Changing Workbook by John Lucht

Building a Great Resume by Kate Wendleton

The $100,000 Resume by Craig Rice

Winning Resumes by Robin Ryan

Guerrilla Marketing by Jay Conrad Levinson

Guerrilla Advertising by Jay Conrad Levinson

101 Ways to Promote Your Web Site by Susan Sweeney
The Self-Publishing Manual by Dan Poynter
1001 Ways to Market Your Books by John Kremer
77 No Talent, No Experience and (Almost) No Cost
   Businesses You Can Start Today! by Kelly Reno
Striking It Rich.com: Profiles of 23 Incredibly Successful Websites
   You've Probably Never Heard Of by Jaclyn Easton
121 Internet Businesses You Can Start From Home by Ron
   E. Gielgun
Success For Less: 100 Low-Cost Businesses You Can Start
   Today by Bob and Terry Adams

Reference Books

Thomas Register of American Manufacturers (annual)
Dun and Bradstreet Million Dollar Directory (annual)
Directory of Corporate Affiliations (annual)
Reference Book of Corporate Managements (annual)
The Career Guide: Dun's Employment Opportunities
   Directory (annual)
Encyclopedia of Associations: National Organizations of the
   U.S.
National Trade and Professional Associations of the U.S.
The Directory of Executive Recruiters (annual)
The Writer's Market (annual)

Websites

Computer Training

New Horizons Computer Learning Center
www.newhorizons.com
1-800-PC-LEARN (1-800-725-3276)

ExecuTrain
www.executrain.com
1-800-90-TRAIN (1-800-908-7246)

Free Internet-Based Courses
www.free-ed.net.
www.webmonkey.com

Management Training
American Management Association
www.amanet.org
1-800-262-9699

Society for Human Resource Management
www.shrm.org
1-703-548-3440

College Degrees
Regents College
www.regents.edu
1-888-647-2388

Thomas Edison University
www.tesc.edu
1-609-292-6565

Distance Degrees Book
www.collegeathome.com
1-541-459-9384

Examination Programs
GRE
www.gre.org
1-609-771-7670

CLEP
www.collegeboard.org/clep
1-609-771-7865

Regents College Exams
www.regents.edu
1-888-RC-EXAMS (1-888-723-9267)

Salary Surveys
www.salary.com
www.careerjournal.com
www.jobstar.org

**Free Market Evaluation and Resume Critique
(also paid resume writing, consulting, and
direct mail services)**
WSA Corp
www.wsacorp.com
1-800-WSA-CORP (1-800-972-2677)

**Free Computer-Based Market Valuation
(must be making $50,000 or more):**
www.futurestep.com

Overtime Exemption Information
Department of Labor Wage and Hour Division
referral line
www.dol.gov
1-866-4-USWAGE

Resume Writing Service
www.resume.com

Job Posting Sites
www.vault.com
www.monster.com
www.headhunter.net
www.employment911.com
www.6figurejobs.com

Computer Industry Jobs
www.dice.com
www.itcareers.com

Human Resource Jobs
www.jobs4hr.com
www.hrworld.com

Construction Trade Jobs
www.tradejobsonline.com

Resume Distribution Service
www.resumezapper.com

Executive Search/Resume, Direct Mail and Consulting Service
www.wsacorp.com
1-800-WSA-CORP (1-800-972-2677)

Free E-Mail Accounts
www.jobmail.net
www.mailcity.com

Information on Getting Free Publicity
Joan Stewart, The Publicity Hound
www.publicityhound.com
1-262-284-7451

Trade Associations
www.associationcentral.com

Management Consultant Referral Service
www.cx.com

Freelance Work/Contract Assignments
www.guru.com

Website Name Registration
www.123domains.com

Website Hosting
www.valueweb.net

More Information on ADD/ADHD Fraud/Class Action Lawsuit
www.adhdfraud.org
www.ritalinfraud.com

Locate and/or Write to Your Congressmen
www.congress.org

Sites of Interest to Stay-at-Home Moms (or would-be stay-at-home moms):
www.athomemothers.com
www.stayathomemom.com
www.momsonline.com
www.momsclub.org
www.homebodies.org
www.mainstreetmom.com

Organizations of Interest to Stay-at-Home Moms
International Moms Club
(over 1,200 chapters)
www.momsclub.org
25371 Rye Canyon
Valencia, CA 91355

National Association of At-Home Mothers
www.athomemothers.com
406 East Buchanan Avenue
Fairfield, IA 52556

Index

About the Author

Joanne Watson is a stay-at-home mom with three children (two boys and a girl). Thanks to Team Work, her husband is now a senior executive at a large and successful hi-tech company earning a six-figure income.